little blessings
from a big God

finding more
of God through
the lives of your children

Michelle Medlock Adams

WHITE STONE BOOKS
LAKELAND, FLORIDA

09 08 07 06   2 3 4 5 6 7 8 9 10

Little Blessings from a Big God
—Finding More of God Through the Lives of Your Children
ISBN 1-59379-020-1
Copyright © Michelle Medlock Adams

Published by White Stone Books
P.O. Box 2835
Lakeland, Florida 33806

little blessings
from a big God

finding more
of God through
the lives of your children

Michelle Medlock Adams

Dedicated to my precious daughters,

Abby Leigh and Allyson Michelle

My daily inspiration

MY GIFTS FROM UP ABOVE

abby and allyson adams

My love for you grows *with each day.*
You've made my life complete,
my precious little baby girls,
so innocent and sweet.

You are the perfect works *of art,*
formed by the Master's touch.
You've taught me how to truly love,
you've given me so much.

Each time I hold *you in my arms,*
the world just fades away.
You're like two tiny rays of sun
who brighten every day.

How could I *want for any more*
when I've been given you?
I know that I am very blessed—
You are my dream come true.

Forever, *I'll thank God for you*
and shower you with love.
Because I know you're heaven-sent,
my gifts from up above.

michelle medlock adams

acknowledgments

Writing this book was an awesome journey, one I didn't go alone. For that reason, I could not let it go to press without thanking those in my life who made the journey possible.

To my Heavenly Father, I give praise and honor! Without You, I am nothing. Thank You for choosing me to be Abby and Allyson's mother. Thank You for loving me enough to teach me, correct me, and guide me on this journey. And thank You for giving me the words to write this book.

To my parents, Walter and Marion Medlock, who not only gave me life, but a Christian home and a firm foundation in the Lord, I give my eternal gratitude. Mom, thank you for always supporting and encouraging me and for the many hours of proofreading rough drafts. And Dad, even though you are no longer on this earth, you were a constant source of unconditional love and approval and I miss you dearly.

To my wonderful husband, Jeff, words cannot express how much I love and appreciate you. I may be the dreamer, but you are the dream maker. Thank you for being my biggest cheerleader when I was having an off day. Thank you for keeping the vision before me when I couldn't see it. Thank you for being a wonderful father to our girls. And, most of all, thank you for being by my side as we journey through life together. You make everything better. I love you.

foreword

As a busy wife and mother of three, I know how hectic life can be at times. With an eleven-year-old playing on two basketball teams, a three- and four-year-old playing pranks on each other, and a husband I often compare to Rambo (without even mentioning the other 1,000 demands of my life), this Copeland house can get a little crazy!

Some days, it is hard just to find quiet time to spend with God, yet it's absolutely necessary if I am going to be the wife, mother, and speaker that God has called me to be. Michelle's book touches this very challenge.

She wrote this book as a result of her heartfelt desire to spend time with God and walk in His wisdom—and she addresses the challenge of doing just that.

Every Mom who has encountered sleepless nights of feeding, changing diapers, and doing endless loads of laundry will find this book an absolute joy!

Michelle writes in a very real way—sharing honestly how God taught her to become more like Him through the lives of her children. One minute you will laugh and the next you will cry. It's the kind of book that you'll take pleasure in reading again and again. I trust you will enjoy the journey of reading this book as much as I did.

Thank you, Michelle, for writing this book for moms everywhere.

Marty Copeland

contents

introduction

I remember the day as though it were yesterday. It was the last day of our senior year of high school, and I was sitting at the lunch table with my best girlfriends in the whole world. Somehow, we knew that life would never be the same after graduation. That realization caused us to begin to talk about some serious issues, such as college, career choices, marriage, and life in general. The more we talked, the more we wondered what the future held for each of us. While speculating about who in the group would get married first, several of my buddies shared their dreams of having a gorgeous, rich husband, a house with a white picket fence and a Jacuzzi, a cute dog, and two or three adorable children. They were all hip on becoming mothers. In fact, some of them had even picked out names for their future offspring. The whole thought of motherhood scared me.

"Not me, I'm never having kids," I said matter-of-factly. "They spit up constantly. They make terrible-smelling messes in their diapers. They cost a lot of money. It'd be like baby-sitting forever. And you never have any time for yourself."

Looking back on those comments, that was a pretty accurate description of motherhood, but only a slight part of it. If I'd known then what I know now, I would not have made the statement, "Not me, I'm never having kids." But I was only eighteen at the time. What did I know?

Now, at age thirty-something, I know that motherhood is the greatest privilege in life. I'm still amazed that I get to be a mom. I certainly didn't earn the right. In fact, I wasn't even excited when I first found out I was pregnant with my oldest daughter, Abby.

It was February 1992.

My husband, Jeff, and I had only been married six months. I had just graduated from Indiana University and landed my first newspaper-reporting job. We'd moved into our own home. We had purchased a miniature dachshund that was trouble enough, but the thought of having a baby was overwhelming! That wasn't supposed to happen until we'd been married at least five years! Not until we had fulfilled some of the other dreams we had for each other as a young married couple.

But God had other plans for me. Don't you know that God has a sense of humor?

Well, whether or not a baby was in our plans, Abby Leigh Adams was born December 3, 1992. All of a sudden, I had this adorable little person to take care of, and I wasn't too skilled at taking care of myself. But God is so good and merciful. He helped me every step of the way, and, of course, Jeff and my mother helped a lot, too.

After a while, I began to like motherhood. In fact, I liked it so much I wanted another baby. And on August 15, 1994, Allyson Michelle Adams joined our family. God had blessed us with two precious daughters, and I still didn't have a clue what I was doing.

Trying to juggle a career, be a wife, learn the skills of motherhood, fulfill church commitments, and still find time to shower once a day was becoming more than I could handle. With all of the extra responsibilities, I felt that my life was beginning to unravel. There were days when I cried out to God, "Are You sure I can do this? You've known me all my life. You know my limitations. Are You sure I'm equipped to handle this motherhood role?"

As the demands on me became more pressing, my daily devotional time became almost nonexistent. By the time I opened my Bible at the end of the day, I was too tired to hear God's voice. Finally, I said to Him one day, "I know I haven't been spending much time with You, but there isn't any time. I can't spend two hours a day in my prayer closet. I have too much to do. If You want to talk to me, You're going to have to do it some other way."

Then I drifted off to sleep, never giving what I'd prayed about much thought after that. I'd said it out of all the frustration and guilt that had built up inside me. I didn't think God would take me seriously, but He did. He started talking to me all the time. Now, I don't mean the skies parted and His thunderous voice filled my house. No, it didn't happen that way. Rather, He began teaching me lessons He wanted me to learn through the lives of my children. Abby or Allyson would say something or do something, and God would speak to me about it. Sometimes, He'd show me how similar my spiritual behavior was to their natural behavior. Other times, He'd simply challenge me to grow in a particular area. I didn't have to attend Bible school every day. God was giving me my own Bible courses—specifically tailored to my needs and shortcomings.

Later, after the girls were a little older, I was asked to co-teach a women's Bible study at our church. I humbly agreed, but inside I felt totally unqualified for the position. I thought, *What could I possibly teach these women? I don't even know what I'm doing half the time. I don't have any great wisdom or insight to share with them.*

Then I heard the Holy Spirit say, *No, but I do. Teach them what I have been teaching you.*

That I could do. So I went to the Bible study every Tuesday and told on myself. That's right. I told them how

God had shown me that I needed to trust Him with everything in my life through an experience I'd had with Abby the week before. Then I told them how God had corrected me for gossiping—also brought to my attention through a parenting experience. Lesson by lesson, I learned more about God through the lives of my children. As I was willing to obey the Holy Spirit and be vulnerable about my personal experiences, I discovered that I wasn't the only one going through those struggles. Soon others opened up and shared that they were having similar challenges. Something special that only God could have done started happening with all of us. Together we began to grow as God showed us practical ways to handle all that we faced as new mothers.

After we moved from that city, I had to give up the Bible study, but the lessons kept coming. God has continued teaching me through my children, and all of those little lessons have added up to one big blessing—a deeper and more committed relationship with God.

That's my prayer for you—that you allow the Holy Spirit to teach you little lessons from each story in this book—lessons that will cause you to grow closer to the Lord.

I was thinking of you when I wrote this book. Each time I wrote a story, I imagined us sitting together, drinking a something cold and delicious, eating a chocolate bar, and discussing our wonderful Heavenly Father. This book is meant to minister to you, challenge you, inspire you, and make you smile along the way.

The little lessons that our big God taught me through my children truly became little blessings and have totally changed my life. I pray they change yours, too.

Chapter One

PERFECT

in every
way

Understanding
How Very Much
God Loves You

It was Halloween 1992, and I was eight months pregnant. In fact, my figure rather resembled the large pumpkin on our front porch. I had been eating for two for many months—two chocolates for me, two chocolates for baby. Needless to say, I avoided wearing orange that night.

The pregnancy had gone well, even though I'd had a few minor contractions early on—nothing really to worry about. And I was expecting a baby girl at the end of November. Life was good.

After putting the finishing touches on our dog's clown costume (he was so embarrassed that he hid behind the couch), we were ready to greet the many trick-or-treaters already lurking about the neighborhood.

"Turn on the front porch light," I called to my husband, Jeff, "and I'll get the treat bags."

As I walked into the kitchen, I felt a terrible pain shoot through my belly. Now was a good time to practice the breathing technique I had learned. After a few "hee hee hoos," the contraction was gone.

Must've been the taco pizza I ate earlier, I thought.

A few minutes later, I had another small contraction, but I wasn't too concerned. I continued handing out treat bags, making comments on all of the kids' scary costumes and forcing my dachshund to show off his clown ensemble. But the contractions also continued, and they were becoming more intense.

"Jeff, it's not the pizza. It's the baby!" I groaned as another contraction started. "I think we'd better head for the hospital."

"But it's too early," Jeff said.

"I don't think she knows that," I urged. "Call the doctor and tell him to meet us at the hospital."

Like any expectant mother, I had been reading all the baby books, learning what physical aspect of my baby was developing during each week of my pregnancy. So I knew if I had the baby that night—four weeks early—her lungs might not be fully developed. I was scared, and yet I wanted to have the baby. I felt I was ready.

Besides, the doctor could have misdiagnosed my due date, I reasoned as we hurried and headed for the hospital.

By the time I was in a hospital gown with my feet propped up in stirrups, I was excited about the prospects of having my baby girl. I knew she would be small, but I also knew that as far along as I was in my pregnancy, she had a great chance of being born perfectly normal.

My parents, Jeff's parents, the extended family, and my best friend had all gathered in the waiting room. With each contraction, I was becoming more excited.

Jeff will have to finish the nursery this weekend, I thought. *And Mom will have to buy some preemie outfits. I just can't wait to hold my baby and cuddle the one who has been kicking me all these months. I can't wait to...*

"Michelle," the doctor said, interrupting my thoughts. "We want to keep this baby inside of you as long as possible because that's best for the baby. I'm going to give you some medication to try to stop your contractions. I need you to lie on your side and try to relax."

"*Stop* my contractions, why?" I whined. "I thought I was going to have this baby tonight. Please, Doc, can't I have her tonight?"

"Not if I can help it," he said, patting me on the head.

Within the next two hours, all of my contractions had stopped. The medicine had worked and I was bummed. After the doctor was assured that the baby was fine, I waddled out of the hospital bed, got dressed, and we headed home. Disappointed that I hadn't given birth, I sat down and finished off the last of the Halloween candy. The doctor had ordered strict bed rest, so I was unable to do much of anything for fear that my labor would start again. And I had to take medication for the next four weeks to keep my contractions from coming.

My life was put on hold. With every passing day, I lay on the couch and envisioned what my daughter would look like, how she would smell, what cute baby sounds she would make, how I would dress her in frilly, pink outfits. I thought about her constantly—except for the moments I thought about mint chocolate chip ice cream. I wanted to have her so badly that it hurt. I even missed a few doses of medication on purpose, hoping to go into labor.

I cried out to God, "C'mon, God. Start my labor. I want to have this baby. Please don't make me wait any longer."

Finally, the day came when I was taken off of bed rest and the labor-stopping medication. I was thirty-eight weeks pregnant and out of the danger zone. I celebrated the day with a shopping trip and a pepperoni pizza. I was absolutely sure that by nightfall I'd be at the hospital in hard labor.

That night the clock ticked more loudly than ever before. Hour after hour. Sitcom after sitcom. Chocolate after chocolate. No contractions. No baby.

I'm never going to have this baby, I thought. *That medication will probably stay in my system and cause me to be pregnant forever.*

Day after day, friends would call and ask, "Any contractions?"

"No."

"Have you tried running up and down the stairs? You might try taking some castor oil. I hear that helps to start contractions."

"Yeah, thanks," I'd mumble.

Each day I had to wait seemed like an eternity. This definitely wasn't how I had planned it would happen. By now I was eight days overdue. Soon the days turned into weeks. I hadn't seen my feet in months. Even my stretch marks had stretch marks. I had run up and down the stairs so many times that my calf muscles were bulging like every other part of my body. I was a total mess— physically and emotionally.

Finally the doctor decided to induce labor. Hallelujah!

My clothes had been packed for so long that they had permanent wrinkles, but I didn't care. I was going to the hospital to have a baby. Life was starting to look good again.

By 4:38 P.M. on December 3, Abby Leigh Adams entered the world, weighing 7 lbs. 5 oz. It had been a difficult pregnancy but an easy birth. As I held Abby for the first time, I marveled over her perfection. From her little pointy head to her long monkey toes, every part of her was perfectly formed.

"You were worth the wait," I whispered to Abby as I kissed her head for the very first time. "You are perfect in every way."

I've often reflected on that long waiting period—from Halloween to December 3. It was one of the most difficult times in my life. Yes, the bed rest was uncomfortable and the contractions were irritating, but those things weren't the cause of my pain. I was simply mad because I hadn't gotten my way and given birth on Halloween. I so wanted to have my baby in October, and when that didn't happen, I was disappointed and miserable. Was that immature? Absolutely. But at the time I didn't think so. I simply wanted to realize my dream of having a baby. I didn't consider all of the other factors.

Isn't that how we act with God sometimes? He puts a dream within our hearts, we lay hold of that dream, and then we try to give birth to it before its appointed time. We don't consider all the factors. We just want to birth that dream and get on with it. Just as I ran up and down the stairs trying to activate my labor, we do silly things to speed up the dream-birthing process. That's so much easier than waiting on God's perfect timing, isn't it? But God knows what's best for us, so in His wisdom, He waits until everything is in place.

Abby would have encountered some serious health challenges if I'd had her too early. Likewise, our dreams can suffer if we try to give birth to them before their appointed time. So, wait on God and His perfect timing. Then, when it's time to birth the dream He has placed inside of you, you'll be able to embrace it and say, "You've been worth the wait. You are perfect in every way."

THOUGHT for the day: Do you have a dream that you're trying to birth prematurely? Are you willing to wait for God's perfect timing?

SCRIPTURE reading: Genesis 15:1-6; 21:1-4; Isaiah 40:31.

DAILY declaration: Father, I ask that You help me to be patient as I wait for Your perfect timing. I thank You for putting dreams in my heart and mind, and I believe that You will cause them to come forth at the appointed time.

Chapter Two

YOU CAN'T

always get
what you
want

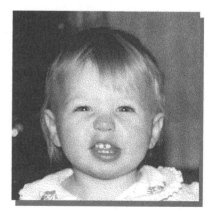

Learning That
God Knows Best

"This is it!" I called to Jeff as he wandered into the kitchen the morning of August 15, 1994.

"This is what?" he mumbled as he drank from the orange juice carton.

"I'm in labor!" I yelled, trying to breathe as I'd learned in Lamaze class. "Get the suitcase. I'll meet you in the car."

Ten minutes later, we were zipping down the highway. We dropped off our eighteen-month-old daughter with my mother. Then we headed toward the hospital, which was more than thirty minutes away.

Just then my water broke.

"Oh no!" I said, staring at the mess on the floor of our Ford Explorer. "We're not going to make it to the hospital in time. She's coming too fast!"

"Oh, man, I just cleaned those floor mats," Jeff teased.

After shooting him a dagger look out of the corner of my eye, I began praying.

"Oh, God, please don't let me have this baby in the car."

Labor had come on quickly. My contractions had started at five minutes apart. Since this was my second child, my body knew what to do, and it was doing it in a hurry. The only problem was, we were still fifteen minutes from the hospital.

My contractions had progressed to two minutes apart, and they were incredibly hard. I had never felt pain like that before. During my labor with Abby, the doctor had given me an epidural before the really difficult labor had ever begun. Her birth had been very easy. I was supposed to have an epidural again with this birth. We'd discussed it in detail with my doctor. I'd signed all the papers.

If I can just make it to the hospital, they can give me an epidural to get rid of this pain, and then I can have my baby, I thought.

Jeff drove like a madman, blowing his horn and flashing his lights at slow-moving motorists. Finally, we arrived at the hospital in Bloomington, Indiana. In his panic-stricken mode, Jeff didn't even think to take me to the emergency room entrance. Nope, instead, he drove to the parking garage, dropped me off at the entrance, and took off to park.

I couldn't believe it. I was in such excruciating pain that I could hardly stand up. The contractions were coming so hard and close together, I was afraid the baby would just fall out right there.

As he squealed around the corner to park our vehicle, I lay down at the entrance next to the double doors that open automatically. I couldn't make it any farther. Still doing my Lamaze breathing and crying at the same time, I lay there in hopes someone would find me. As big as I had gotten, I would be hard to miss. That was in my favor.

Sure enough, a nurse going off duty saw me lying there and immediately called for a wheelchair. She also had the foresight to call the OB floor to let them know I was on my way. As she helped me into the wheelchair, I begged, "Could you get me some drugs? I need some painkiller right way."

She smiled graciously and tried to comfort me as she pushed me into the hospital.

Meanwhile, Jeff couldn't find me. He remembered leaving me at the door, but I was nowhere to be found by the time he got back from parking the Explorer. Eventually, he made his way to the OB floor, bypassing all of the normal, necessary paperwork because of how far along my labor had progressed.

When we finally reached the maternity ward, I couldn't believe my eyes. The ward was full. Every birthing room was occupied, and some moms-to-be were out in the hallway concentrating on doing their Lamaze breathing correctly.

This is not looking good, I thought, wincing in pain as another hard contraction started. *I'm going to have to birth this baby in a closet somewhere.*

Instead, they wheeled one expectant mom out of Birthing Room #9 and wheeled me right past her. We smiled at each other in between our "hoo, hoo, hee" breaths, and the next thing I knew, I was in a gown and my legs were propped up in stirrups.

Just then I saw Jeff in the hallway and hollered for him.

"Honey, get the doctor and tell him I need my epidural right away. I can't stand this pain anymore."

Jeff pulled a nurse to the side and explained to her that I was supposed to have an epidural the same as I'd had with my first child. Then I heard a lot of whispering. Never a good sign.

"Sweetheart," Jeff said, stroking my hair, "the nurse said you're going to have this baby very, very soon, and there wouldn't be time for an epidural."

"What do you mean!" I screamed in despair. "The doctor said I could have one! You get that doctor in here and tell him I want my epidural *now*! We had an agreement! I signed the papers! It's official!"

The nurse looked at Jeff. Jeff looked at the nurse. Both of them looked at me, and I added, "I will never forgive you if you don't find my doctor and get me that epidural!"

Jeff left the room in search of the doctor, so he said. (I think he really went to get a cup of coffee. I'll never know for sure.) Anyway, that left me alone with my attending nurse. She was a young, pretty woman. She spoke in a gentle voice and smiled a lot. All of which was really irritating me. I motioned for her to come to my side, and then I did something I'm not very proud of. I grabbed her little nurse's outfit with both fists, pulled her toward me, and said, "Please, for the love of God, get me some drugs right now!"

She took my hands in hers, squeezed them tenderly, and said, "I'm going to leave you for a minute while I get the doctor to check your progress. It'll all be over soon."

Yeah, easy for YOU to say, I thought. *You're not in excruciating pain.*

My doctor had just come on duty and hadn't even had time to change into scrubs. He quickly examined me and said, "Oh, my. That baby's coming like a freight train."

"And it feels like one, too," I said. "Could you get me an epidural for the pain, Doc?"

As he slipped on a gown over his clothes, he explained in great detail that I was too far along in labor for an epidural.

"In fact," he said, "any pain medication I give you now will directly affect the baby. You're going to have to do this the old-fashioned way. The good news is, you, Mama, are ready to push."

That was not what I wanted to hear. But at least he told me I could push. That was the only bright spot of the whole painful ordeal.

Four pushes later, I had a baby—Allyson Michelle Adams.

As Jeff cut the umbilical cord, I thanked God for my precious baby girl. She was perfect, and I was done. I'd given birth naturally, without any drugs. Of course, this wasn't by choice, but at any rate, I had survived it. I felt like Superwoman, only a little meaner.

"That's how I like to see a baby born—like a freight train," the doctor commented as he finished attending to me. I gave him a half smile and exhaled a big sigh of relief.

All of the grandparents and the rest of the family made it to the hospital just in time to see baby Allyson in her new pink toboggan as the nurse cleaned her and weighed her.

It was a joyous occasion. And even though I had acted absolutely awful, my kind attending nurse brought me a soda and congratulated me on the birth of my daughter.

Later, as I lay in my hospital room holding my baby girl, I replayed the morning's ordeal in my mind. I wrote the attending nurse an "I'm sorry" note for grabbing her and screaming in her face, and then I nursed my new baby. Life was good. All was well.

Looking back, I learned a lot of valuable lessons from the birth of my second daughter. The main lesson I learned was this: You can't always get what you want. If I had received an epidural as I'd requested, it could have been harmful to the baby. It wouldn't have helped my pain. By the time the effect of the painkiller would've kicked in, the baby would have already been born. But I didn't know those things. All I knew was I had an immediate need and I wanted something to fill it. I wasn't concerned about the details. I just wanted some relief from my pain.

Isn't that exactly how we are in our dealings with God?

We want immediate relief from our pain—we don't care how we get that relief; we just want it now! There have been times in my life when I was hurting so badly inside that I thought I would die. During my prayer time I wanted to grab God by His collar, just as I had that nurse, and scream, "Father, make the pain go away now!"

I discovered through the birth of my second daughter that God's timing is perfect. No matter how much we beg, demand, cry, or whine. He always has our best interest at heart. He looks for ways to bless us because He loves us so much.

God knows the future. In fact, it tells us in Psalm 139:16-18 that He scheduled each day of our lives before we were born. That's comforting to me. Somehow it takes all the pressure off, knowing that He's got it all under control. When my days seem hectic and filled with too much to do, I remind myself that God is looking out for me. The Bible says that He knows the number of hairs on our head, so there is no detail of life that doesn't concern Him.

If your prayers aren't being answered, or some situation isn't working out as you'd hoped, follow these steps. First, make sure that you are totally sold out to Jesus, holding back nothing from Him. Second, make sure that you aren't in strife with anyone or harboring any unforgiveness in your heart, because the Word tells us that those wrong attitudes will hinder our prayers. And, third, find scriptures in the Word that pertain to your situation. If you can find it in the Word, you've got great ammunition to take to prayer. Finally, rest in Him, knowing that He has the perfect answer for you, even if it's not the one you've been praying for. It may not always happen the way you expected, but you'll always get the best if you'll let God have His way. That's a promise.

THOUGHT for the day: God knows what's best for you, so listen for His answer.

SCRIPTURE reading: Psalm 139:16-18; Isaiah 55:8-9; Matthew 6:7-8; Hebrews 13:6.

DAILY declaration: I trust You, Lord. Even when Your answer isn't the one I wanted, I still trust You and Your plan because I know You love me.

Chapter Three

you always

PROMISE!

Being Faithful
to Your Word
and the Word

The pile of work on my desk had grown so high that I could barely see over the top of it. Deadlines, deadlines, and more deadlines.

How am I ever going to finish all of this by next week? I wondered.

After prioritizing the stack of assignments in front of me, I took a snack break with Abby and Allyson, then ages five and three. We piled cheese atop crackers and munched until there were crumbs all over the kitchen table. It was great fun, but I had work awaiting me.

"Mommy's got to work, so I want you two to watch a video while I get some stuff finished, okay?"

"But I thought you were going to take us to the park!" Abby protested. "You said you would. You promised!"

"Yes, yes I did promise, and I'll take you just as soon as I finish this one project," I negotiated. "I promise."

Abby put her pouty face back in her bag of tricks and headed for the playroom where Allyson was already absorbed in her favorite movie, *Cinderella.*

Minutes turned to hours as I pecked away at the computer keyboard. I worked through dinner and bath time—both handled by Daddy. Just as I put the final touches on my assignment, I saw a pair of green eyes peering at me over the top of my work pile.

"Whatcha doin', Ab?" I asked.

Silence.

"Did you put some of Mommy's smelly lotion on after your bath?"

Silence.

"What's wrong, sweetie?" I asked innocently.

"You didn't take us to the park!" she said.

Disappointment was written all across her face. I sighed and sunk into my chair, realizing I had let them down once again.

"Well, Mommy didn't realize her work would take so long tonight," I explained. "But I have a good start on this work pile, so I'll take you tomorrow after school. I promise."

"You *always promise!*" Abby said, then turned and walked away from me.

Her words hurt, but I knew in my heart she was right. I did always promise. I didn't mean to break my promises. When I made them, I had every intention of keeping my word, but I rarely did. I felt such sadness in my heart.

Now what do I do? I asked myself.

I saved my work on the computer and cowered into the girls' rooms, just as our dogs do when they've had an accident on the carpet. If I'd had a tail, it would have been tucked between my legs.

"Good night, my precious girls," I whispered, kissing them one by one.

Daddy had already said their evening prayers with them, so there was nothing left for me to do except turn off their lights and hope for a better tomorrow. As I headed back down the hallway, I heard voices coming from the playroom. It was *Cinderella*. The movie was

playing for the third consecutive time that night. Only
this time, there was no audience.

I plopped down on the sofa and watched as Cinderella
did chore after chore so that she could attend the grand
ball. As she floated down the stairs in the pink ball gown
that the mice had created for her, she called after her
stepmother and stepsisters, "Please wait for me."

They glared at her, and the stepsisters began to whine
to their mother about letting Cinderella attend the ball.
But the wicked stepmother said, "We did have a bargain,
didn't we, Cinderella? And I never go back on my word."

Those words echoed in my ears. I'd seen that Disney
classic dozens of times before, but I'd never heard those
words as I heard them that night. Suddenly, they took on
new meaning as I watched the mean-spirited stepsisters
rip Cinderella's dress to shreds, leaving her alone in rags
while they left for the ball.

I grabbed the remote control and hit the rewind
button. As the movie rewound, so did my mind. Memory
after memory flooded my thoughts and reminded me of
the many times I had promised something to Abby and
Allyson, never made good on my word, and then
explained my way out of it. I'd used every excuse in the
book, but in reality, there was no excuse. I realized that I
had been a poor reflection of God to my children.

*If they can't believe me and my word, how will they ever
believe God and His promises?* I thought.

I determined in my heart that night that I would
never again make a promise I couldn't keep. I prayed for
forgiveness and asked the Lord to help me be a better
reflection of Him in the area of keeping promises.

"No more excuses," I prayed. "I repent for breaking so many promises to my children and ultimately to You, Lord."

The next morning, I pushed my pile of work aside and planned a special day for my girls. We had what is now affectionately known as a "Mommy Day"—a day where it's just me and the girls, doing fun girl stuff. We shopped, ate ice cream, and visited a nearby park. No, that didn't make up for all of my broken promises, but God forgave me and so did my girls. And just like *Cinderella*, we had a happy ending.

If you struggle in the area of keeping promises, don't beat yourself up about it. Make a quality decision to change. It's not too late. Tell the Lord you are sorry and ask Him to forgive you. Then receive His forgiveness and go on. Ask Him to help you become more realistic in this area. He wants to help. All you have to do is ask, and He will be with you every step along the path to fulfilling your word and also to help you avoid overcommitment. You have my word on that, and that's a promise I can keep!

THOUGHT for the day: Have you been overcommitting and breaking promises to those you love? Have you been breaking promises to God?

SCRIPTURE reading: Romans 12:1-2; 2 Corinthians 7:1; Galatians 3:29.

DAILY declaration: Father, I choose today to begin again with You. I believe that You have forgiven me and placed my broken promises in the sea of forgetfulness, and I thank You for it. Help me to be a better reflection of You in every aspect of my life.

Chapter Four

EVERY DOG

has its day

Choosing God
Over Everything Else

"Allyson, come on, let's go, honey," I called to my four-year-old daughter.

After giving every child in the preschool a hug good-bye, Allyson scampered over to where I was waiting.

"Okay, I'm ready now," she informed me.

As we rounded the corner toward the exit, I noticed a bright-colored sign on the bulletin board. It read, "Dress like the family member you most admire this Friday."

"That's *tomorrow!*" I mumbled to myself, already thinking of how I could dress Allyson to look like me.

I've got the perfect little blue scarf that I could tie around her neck, I thought. *And, of course, I could pull her hair into a professional-looking clip. Yes, and I'll have her wear navy pants and a crisp, white shirt. Maybe I'll put a pencil behind her ear and let her carry a reporter's notebook. I'll even let her wear a little bit of makeup. She'll look so cute!*

As I loaded Allyson into the backseat, she gave me a kiss on the cheek.

"Thank you," I said, buckling her seatbelt. "What was that for?"

"For being the bestest mommy in the world," she answered.

"Good answer," I teased.

After hearing all about how Gabriel chased her around the playground and tried to kiss her that afternoon, our conversation turned to Friday's Dress-Up Day.

"Ally, I read where you are supposed to dress up tomorrow like the person in your family that you most admire. Are you going to do it?"

"Yep," she said. "I wanted to go dressed as a princess, but the Teacher said I couldn't."

I just had to ask, even though I already knew the answer.

"So *who* are you going to dress up like?" I smugly asked, peering at her in the rearview mirror.

Allyson looked up at me with those big blue eyes and said sweetly, "Maddie."

"*Maddie!*" I shrieked. "But Maddie is a dog! You can't dress up like our *dog*!"

"But I want to dress up like Maddie! I love Maddie!" Allyson insisted, accompanied by streaming crocodile tears and irregular breathing.

Well, I thought, *I'll be the laughingstock of the daycare. I bet nobody else's daughter will choose the family dog as the family member she most admires. Where did I go wrong? Doesn't she know I have stretch marks because of her! I've earned the right to be the most admired person in her life. What about all of those nights I rocked her to sleep? What about all of the times I kissed her tears and hurts away? What about the endless hours of reading story after story to her? What about...?*

My feel-sorry-for-myself thoughts were interrupted by Allyson's chanting: "I want Maddie. I want Maddie. I want Maddie."

You get the idea.

As we pulled into the driveway of our home, I realized it was time to pull out the big guns—bribery and manipulation.

"Allyson, if you dress up like Mommy, I'll let you wear makeup and perfume!" I coaxed.

"No, I want to be Maddie," she said, breezing past me on her way to see the infamous Maddie—a miniature longhaired dachshund with an attitude twice her size.

As I heard Allyson's giggles and Maddie's excited barks in the other room, I knew I'd had it. Maddie, the little furball, had won. There was no use fighting it anymore. I'd lost the title of "Most Admired" to a weiner dog.

There was nothing left to do except admit defeat and make the Maddie costume.

I found some faux fur left over from Halloween pasts. "This should be perfect," I said as I grabbed some wire and my hot-glue gun.

For the next two hours, I slaved over that dog costume. It was no longer an activity to help my daughter. It was a personal mission now. If she was going to dress up like the family dog, she was going to be the best-looking pup in the preschool.

I took a break from my masterpiece-creating long enough to feed Allyson supper, give her a bubble bath, read her a story, say a bedtime prayer, and tuck her into bed. At 9:30 P.M., I was a glue-gunning fool once again. At about 11:30 P.M., I finished what will forever be known as the best designer dog costume ever created by amateur hands.

Through bloodshot eyes I proudly looked at the
furry ears and tail I'd made and decided to call it a night.

The next morning we were up early. It would take
extra time to get ready for the big day. I still wasn't sure
exactly how I was going to pin the costume to Ally's
black bodysuit or make the dog collar fit her neck
without choking her. As I carefully pinned the furry
creation to Allyson's body, she giggled and wiggled. I
gently secured the dog ears to Ally's fine blond hair and
completed Ally's look by painting her nose all black—just
like Maddie's.

When I'd finished, Allyson stepped in front of the
full-length mirror and gave her best "bark."

"I really look like Maddie, don't I, Mommy?" she asked.

"You sure do," I said, hurriedly applying my mascara
as we raced out the door.

On the drive to the preschool, I couldn't help but
glance at Allyson in the rearview mirror every few
seconds. She looked so cute and so pleased with herself.
I, on the other hand, was mortified. Yes, I knew it was
prideful to feel the way I felt, but I couldn't fight my
emotions.

*How could I lose to a dog? Why wouldn't she choose me?
I'm so good to her*, I thought.

Then I heard that inward voice speaking to me.

I'm good to you all the time, but you don't always choose Me.
Ouch.

I knew the Holy Spirit's words were true. And just in
case I needed further explanation, the Lord took me
back to the weekend before when I'd chosen to sleep in

instead of going to Sunday school, as well as Saturday night when I'd neglected my quiet time with the Lord to watch a movie I'd rented.

I swallowed hard and let out a big sigh.

"I'm sorry, Lord. I had no idea how often I choose something over You. Please forgive me," I mumbled as I headed down the street to Ally's preschool.

As we pulled into the preschool's drive, I noticed all the other little girls walking into the building, hand in hand with their mommies. Every single one of them was dressed like her mother. Some wore rollers and aprons. Others carried briefcases and wore tiny little suits. But all were obviously miniature mommies—all but *my* daughter. I sighed a big sigh and swallowed my pride as I walked Allyson up to the door. I could see several mothers congregated outside the building turn and look in our direction.

As we walked past the group of mommies, one of them called out, "And who are you supposed to be, honey?"

Allyson smiled up at the woman and said, "I'm Maddie. She's my dog."

The woman chuckled to herself, and the other mommies chimed in with their chortles.

"Well, you are a very beautiful dog," the woman added.

Then Allyson said something I'll never forget as long as I live.

"Thank you," she said. "My mommy made my costume because she's the bestest mommy in the whole world."

With that, Allyson kissed me good-bye, leaving a black smudge on my face and a warm feeling in my heart.

I knew Allyson loved me, but it sure was nice to hear her announce it in her sweet, genuine way.

Our Heavenly Father likes to hear us tell Him how much we adore Him, too. Sometimes our choices may not show our love for God. I know I am still challenged in this area. But even when our choices aren't perfect, God still loves us. The same way I loved Allyson, even though she chose a weiner dog over me.

Why not take some time today and evaluate the choices you've made over the past week? Were they good ones? Did you spend time with God each day? Is He at the top of your list or somewhere near the bottom? When was the last time you told Him how much you loved Him?

THOUGHT for the day: Do your choices genuinely reflect what's in your heart?

SCRIPTURE reading: Psalms 27:4; 34:1; 119:96-97; 3 John 11.

DAILY declaration: I choose You, God, over everything else. I love You, Lord, and I want all of my choices to reflect the love that I have for You.

Chapter Five

DON'T BE

fooled by
pretty weeds

Letting God
Weed Your Garden

One afternoon as my daughter Abby was playing outside, she discovered a patch of purple weeds growing in the middle of my beautiful begonias. Abby picked one of the weeds and brought it to me.

"Here, Mommy. I picked you a flower," she said enthusiastically.

I smiled and graciously accepted it. As I looked at the weed more closely, I thought, *My, this weed really is lovely. It could almost fool anybody into thinking it's a flower.*

I decided that it was time to weed my flower bed—no matter how pretty those purple weeds were.

Later that evening, I received a telephone call from a friend at church. She began sharing some damaging information about a person in our congregation. I listened for a while because my friend kept interjecting, "I'm just telling you all of this so that you'll know how to pray about it." But the longer she went on, the more I felt uncomfortable in my spirit. Somehow, what she was saying about that other person didn't seem right. I hung up the receiver and felt dirty on the inside.

"Man, I wish I hadn't been a part of that," I mumbled.

As conviction did its job on my conscience, I went into my bedroom and got down on my knees.

"God, I'm sorry I was a part of that. I should have identified that information as gossip the moment she started."

I stayed on my knees in silence, feeling really bad about that evening's conversation. I replayed it over and over in my mind. Just then, God brought to my remembrance the purple weed Abby had given me just hours before.

That pretty purple weed that fooled Abby fooled you, too, God spoke into my spirit.

I knew just what He meant.

That gossip I had just heard was packaged nicely with, "I'm just sharing this information with you so that you'll know how to pray about it." It was a pretty purple weed. But weeds are weeds and gossip is gossip. Both choke out life.

That little weed that looked so innocent and pretty among my begonias would have eventually choked the life right out of them if I hadn't weeded my flower bed that afternoon. And if we continue to let little weeds like gossip grow in our lives, they'll soon overtake us, too.

When the Holy Spirit prompts you to pick some weeds in your life, pray about it and ask for divine wisdom and discernment. The big ugly weeds are easy to identify. It's the attractive ones we have to worry about. Let God be the ultimate Gardener in your life. As you live close to Him, you'll become more skilled at identifying the weeds in your life—even the pretty ones.

THOUGHT for the day: Do you have any weeds in your life? How long has it been since you asked God to weed the garden of your heart with His Word?

SCRIPTURE reading: Proverbs 11:13; 16:28; James 1:22, chapter 3.

DAILY declaration: Father, I want You to weed my garden that I might grow in You. Help me, Lord, to identify the areas in my life that need work. I am committed to keeping my garden beautiful, full of life, and thriving in You.

Chapter Six

DO YOU
trust me?

Learning to
Trust God
in Every Situation

It was a dark and rainy night as I drove home from a nearby city. My daughter Abby was three and a half at the time. She lay asleep in her carseat next to me. Because of the bad weather, I decided to bypass the usual way and take a different, more lighted road home. Just as I whipped our SUV in a different direction, Abby woke up.

"We're lost, aren't we, Mommy?" she asked.

"No, honey. Mommy's just taking a different route home tonight," I replied. "I know what I'm doing. Not to worry."

I could see the doubt in Abby's eyes as headlights from a passing car illuminated our vehicle. After a few more minutes, she asked again, "Are you sure you know what you're doing? I don't think this is the right way," she insisted.

I caringly stroked Abby's hair and said, "Do you trust me enough to try it my way?"

As I uttered those words, conviction covered me like a heavy blanket. The Holy Spirit reminded me how I'd questioned God earlier that week. I knew I was supposed to wait for the freelance job God had promised me, but a good full-time journalistic opportunity was dangling in front of me. I wasn't sure whether or not to take that full-time job and ask God to bless it anyway or wait for the job God had promised me, which seemed impossible to attain. Confirmation after confirmation assured me the freelance job would be mine, but it had been such a long wait.

Maybe God had changed His mind, I'd reasoned earlier that week.

I had cried out, "God, what's going on? The job You promised isn't any closer than it was six months ago. Do You really think I should let this other opportunity pass me by? You know, we're really hurting for money right now. What if I turn down this job and the other one never comes my way?"

Just then, it was as if I saw my Heavenly Father reach down into our SUV and lovingly stroke my hair and say, "Michelle, do you trust Me enough to try it My way?"

As tears streamed down my face, I thanked God for being so patient with my fledgling faith. I promised Him I'd become more like Matthew and follow Him without asking any questions (Matthew 9:9).

The following day I turned down the full-time job that offered an immediate solution to our financial situation, trusting God to perform His Word. And He did— just as He'd promised. Two weeks later that steady freelance opportunity was mine, and it paid even more than I had expected. I was able to work from home and take care of my two little girls.

God always does more than we could ask or think if we'll only trust in Him. Some days I'm better at doing that than others, but I'm learning that God's ways are always better than mine. The Bible says in Isaiah 55:8

that His thoughts are not our thoughts, neither are His ways our ways. It goes on to say in verse 9 that as the heavens are higher than the earth, so are His ways higher than our ways, and His thoughts higher than our thoughts. That's proven true many times in my life. Even when I think I've figured out the situation from every angle, I haven't even scratched the surface of God's infinite wisdom. God always knows best. He only asks us to follow Him. He doesn't ask us to figure it out first, and then follow Him. That's why it's called a walk of faith.

In the same way I had asked Abby to trust me enough to do it my way, God wants us to trust Him enough to do it His way. If we can have enough faith to take the first step down God's path, He'll gently nudge us the rest of the way. He has promised never to leave or forsake us no matter what we face. And at the end of the path, God has our ultimate dream waiting for us. So don't settle for less, and don't give up. Be willing to try it God's way. Our Father really does know best.

THOUGHT for the day: Is there a situation in your life that you're afraid to give to God? Do you trust Him enough to do it His way?

SCRIPTURE reading: Jeremiah 29:11; Matthew 8:21-22; 9:9.

DAILY declaration: I will follow You, Lord. I will trust You in every situation because I know that You have good plans for me. I'm willing to try it Your way today, Father.

Chapter Seven

MOMMY,
that's
Doris Day!

Learning to
Know God's Voice

On rainy days, I love to watch movies with my girls. I pop popcorn—the real buttery kind. We put on our favorite jammies. Then we all pile on my bed, snuggle under the covers, munch popcorn, and watch movies. Sometimes Daddy even joins us.

Occasionally, we watch Disney Classics, such as *Bambi* or *Cinderella*, but most often we watch Doris Day movies. From *That Touch of Mink* to *Pillow Talk* to *With Six You Get Eggroll*—we love them all.

Abby, my oldest daughter, adores Doris Day. She can almost recite *Please Don't Eat the Daisies* by heart, we've watched it so many times. Abby has grown up with Doris Day, Rock Hudson, Cary Grant, and the rest—just as I did.

My mother and I used to pop popcorn, pile on her big bed, snuggle under the covers, and watch Doris Day and Rock Hudson movies on Sunday afternoons. Those times are special memories for me, so I love making those same marvelous movie memories with my daughters. It's become a family tradition, one I'm quite fond of. In fact, we look forward to rainy Saturdays so we can have a "Doris Day" day.

On one such rainy afternoon, we enjoyed a Doris Day double feature. We watched *The Thrill of It All* with Doris Day and James Garner, followed by *Move Over, Darling*, also starring the talented twosome. When the second movie ended, Abby and Allyson retreated to their playroom for some serious playtime before "lights out," while I picked up stray popcorn pieces.

Since it was a weekend, Jeff and I agreed to let the girls sleep in the playroom. That way, they could fall asleep watching a movie. Before I knew it, the hour was 11 P.M. I crawled into bed and drifted off to sleep, dreaming of Jeff, who looked a lot like James Garner in my dreamlike state.

Right in the middle of my dream, I felt hot breath on my cheek. It wasn't the dogs, because they were lying at the foot of the bed. It wasn't Jeff, because he had fallen asleep in the living room recliner. I opened one eye to see Abby standing right over me.

"What do you want, Ab?" I mumbled.

"I want to tell you something," she said with great excitement in her voice.

I figured I'd better open both eyes, since she was obviously not going away until I had heard her most important news.

"What?" I asked.

"I just heard Doris Day at the end of that movie we rented. She's singing some song about rubber tree plants and tight ropes."

Rubber tree plants and tight ropes, I pondered. *Hmmmm.*

"Oh, you mean, rubber tree plants and high hopes!" I said, quite pleased with myself for figuring that one out.

"Yeah, that's it," she beamed. "C'mom, Mommy, you've got to hear it."

So I rolled out of bed, stumbled down the hallway, and poked my head into the playroom long enough to hear Doris Day's beautiful voice singing "High Hopes."

"Yep, that's her!" I assured Abby. "Good ear. I can't believe you knew it was her without even seeing her."

"I know her voice," Abby said quite proudly.

I kissed Abby on the forehead and covered up Allyson, who was already in dreamland, before returning to bed. As I lay there trying to get to sleep again, I thought about what Abby had said—"I know her voice."

At the time, Abby was only six years old, yet I had exposed her to so many Doris Day movies that it took her only seconds to identify Miss Day's voice. She knew it was Doris without even seeing her.

I realized that I had raised a serious Doris Day fan, and that made me smile. But then I thought of something that wiped the smile from my face.

Have I exposed my girls to God's Word enough that they would know His voice that quickly?

Sure, I had taken them to church from the time they were born, but had I really encouraged them to meditate on God's promises? Had I talked enthusiastically about His Word and His blessings as I had talked about Doris Day's career and her movie credits? Could Abby recite scriptures as well as she could recite the words to *Please Don't Eat the Daisies*?

I wasn't sure.

Certainly, there was nothing wrong with our Doris Day movie marathons. I had no guilt over that. But I realized that night that I needed to spend more time encouraging my girls in the Word of God. I needed to be as enthusiastic about God when I talked with the girls as I was when I talked about Doris Day. I knew that if I showed excitement and adoration for God and His ways, they would, too—just as they had followed my lead with Doris Day.

Days later I continued to hear Abby's words, "I know her voice," over and over in my head. It was a constant reminder of the revelation I had that night.

Since then I have made a conscious effort to show my enthusiasm for God. I don't talk about my devotion time as a "have to" obligation anymore. Instead, I let the girls know that Mommy is retreating to her room to have an exciting conversation with the Lord. I no longer find excuses to get out of going to Wednesday night church services. I pick up the girls from school on Wednesdays and start talking about how much fun we're going to have that night at church. Now we pile onto Abby's bed every night, snuggle under the covers, and read from a children's devotional book. Then we all join hands and pray together. That special time is becoming a new family tradition in our home, and I'm so glad to see my children growing closer to the Lord.

I fully expect that my girls will come to know God's voice just as well as they know Doris Day's. Believing that has given me "High Hopes" for my daughters' futures.

THOUGHT for the day: How well do you know God's voice? How well do your children know His voice?

SCRIPTURE reading: Psalm 119:96-105; John 10:1-16; chapter 20.

DAILY declaration: Father, I want to know Your voice. I want to be able to identify it immediately. I want to hear it over all of the other voices in my day-to-day life. Help me to know You more. And, Father, help me to show my enthusiasm for You and Your Word. Let my children see that excitement in me and long for it, too. Amen.

Chapter Eight

DON'T

look behind

the chair!

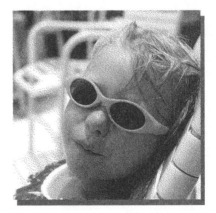

Serving God
Wholeheartedly

As I carried another load of dirty clothes to the laundry room, I glanced inside Abby's and Allyson's rooms. What I saw was scary. Barbie dolls everywhere. Clothes and shoes all over the floor. Dresser drawers halfway open, with clothes spilling out of them. Candy wrappers scattered across their rooms.

It was ultimatum time.

"Okay, here's the deal," I said to the girls, then ages seven and five. "You either clean up your rooms, or we're not going swimming today. That's final. Got it?"

"Yes, ma'am," Abby said, marching off to her room.

Allyson said nothing, following behind her sister.

I finished cleaning up the kitchen, removing sticky Cheerios from our oak table, while Abby and Allyson worked on cleaning their rooms. After a few minutes, Abby sashayed into the kitchen, opened the cabinet below our kitchen sink, and grabbed some glass cleaner.

"I'm gonna clean my mirror," she said. "It's got fingerprints all over it."

I was impressed.

A few minutes later, Allyson bounded into the kitchen with an important announcement.

"I'm finished!" she said, modeling her orange and yellow bathing suit.

"Finished what?" I asked.

"Finished getting ready."

"Finished getting ready for what?"

"To go swimming," she said matter-of-factly.

"Is your room clean?"

"Uh huh," she said, "come see."

So I did. And to my amazement, her bedroom looked really clean. The dresser drawers were shut all the way. The clothes were put away. The shoes were put away. Even the Barbie dolls were gone. I could actually see the carpet. Just as I was about to congratulate Allyson on her clean room, she walked in front of her miniature recliner that sat in the corner of her room and said, "Don't look behind the chair!"

Guilt was written all over her rosy little cheeks.

Playing along, I innocently asked, "Why not?"

"Just don't," she said defensively.

I had no choice. I had to look behind the recliner, and when I did, I saw a pile of clothes, shoes, Barbie dolls, and candy wrappers. She was caught red-handed, and she knew it.

Meanwhile, Abby had truly cleaned her room and was able to watch cartoons while Allyson had to put away the pile of stuff stacked behind her recliner.

She whined and whimpered as she folded clothing, threw out trash, and put away dolls. Then, forty-five minutes later, she finished, and we were able to go to the pool.

Her little act of disobedience had cost us an hour of "pool time." She was sorry, but being sorry couldn't get her back that hour she had lost. It was a good lesson for her, and a good lesson for me, as well.

I thought about how many times in my life I had gone before the Father and said, "I'm finished cleaning up. Come and see, but just don't look behind that chair in the far corner of my heart."

Just as Allyson thought she could fool me, at times I thought I could fool God. And just as Allyson's disobedience had cost her time at the pool, my disobedience had kept me from walking in the fullness of God.

By keeping one part of my heart from Him, I had limited what He could do with me and for me. I could never walk in my true calling if I held back any part of my life from Him. Hiding things from God had cost me more than I wanted to think about.

But there was one difference: I couldn't get that hour of pool time back for Allyson, but God could restore the time that I had wasted in disobedience. And that's exactly what He has done in my life. Every time I pull the old "don't look behind the chair" routine, God patiently waits for me to repent, and then He puts me back on the right road as if I'd never missed a step. That's because He is so merciful and good.

He will do the same for you. So go ahead and get out those stinky, dirty, unsightly, and cluttered items from behind that chair in the corner of your heart and start cleaning today. God's waiting.

THOUGHT for the day: Do you have a mess behind the chair in the far corner of your heart?

SCRIPTURE reading: Hebrews 3:7-12; 5:12-14; 1 John 1:9.

DAILY declaration: Lord, I am tired of hiding things from You. This very day, I give all of my heart to You—even the mess behind the chair in the corner of my heart. I ask that You help me to clean up my act and move forward with You in total obedience and integrity. I love You, Lord.

Chapter Nine

BEING
toothless
isn't so
bad

Trusting God
with Every Part of Your Life

"Stop it, Ally! It's not funny!"

"Is so!" Allyson taunted.

The unpleasant exchange was followed by bursts of squeals and crying. I buried my head under my pillow, hoping to drown out their bickering. It wasn't exactly the way I wanted to begin my Friday.

I peered out from beneath my pillow and looked at the alarm clock through squinted eyes. It was almost time to get up anyway. I rolled out of bed, slipped on my leopard print slippers, and stumbled down the hallway toward the girls' rooms.

"What's going on in here?" I demanded.

"Ally is making fun of my loose tooth," Abby whined.

"Is that true, Allyson?"

She said nothing, indicating her guilt.

"Ally, it isn't nice to make fun of people. Tell your sister you're sorry."

"Sorry," Allyson said with just a twinge of "I'm saying it but I don't really mean it" in her voice.

Abby was satisfied with the apology, and that was good enough for me. Besides, I had breakfast to fix and lunches to pack. As I hurried into the kitchen, Jeff passed me in the hall, giving me a quick good-bye kiss on his way off to work.

"I'll pull that tooth for you tonight," Daddy called to Abby, who was wiggling her loose tooth in the bathroom mirror.

"*No!*" Abby hollered. "I don't want you to."

With lunches packed, bodies dressed, hair combed, teeth brushed, and faces washed, we piled into the car and headed for the elementary school. On the way there, Abby inspected her lunch.

"I can't eat an apple," she said, pointing to a top front tooth that was so loose it was hanging out of her mouth.

As she spoke, the tooth turned and twisted, moving with each word. She looked a little like Snaggletooth. I so wanted to pull that tooth. It was more than ready to come out.

"Sorry, Ab," I said. "Why don't you let me pull that tooth for you, and then you can eat a whole orchard of apples?"

"*No!*" she insisted. "I don't want you to. It's *my* tooth!"

It was Abby's very first loose tooth. She thought it was cool, and she wanted to hang on to that tooth as long as possible.

"You know, Abby, if you let me pull your tooth, you can stick it underneath your pillow tonight, and the tooth fairy will leave you a whole dollar!" I coaxed. "Not only that, you'll get to join the 'Lost Tooth Club' in your class. That's cool, isn't it?"

"Yeah," she said, halfway ignoring me, "but I still don't want you to pull it."

That was it—that was her final answer.

Days passed and that poor little tooth hung on for dear life. Abby was obsessed with keeping that tooth. She carefully avoided the loose tooth while brushing her teeth. She refused to eat anything that required much chewing. And she was constantly wiggling it with her tongue. I just couldn't understand why she liked it so much. It was really becoming an eyesore to me. It gave me the heebie-jeebies just to look at it flopping about in her mouth.

A whole week had gone by, and Snaggletooth still ruled our household. Then one night as I was loading the dishwasher I heard, "Oh no! My tooth! My tooth! *Mom!*"

I dashed out of the kitchen, down the hall, and into Abby's room. There she stood, smiling a toothless grin and holding a sucker with a little tooth stuck to it. That little tooth had fought a good fight, but it lost to a grape lollipop. And I, for one, was eternally grateful.

That night Abby tucked the tooth under her pillow, and a tooth fairy wearing leopard-print slippers delivered the cash. The following day, Abby was inducted into her school's "Lost Tooth Club" and received a special sticker in honor of the most important occasion. From that day on, Abby checked her teeth every day, hoping to find a loose one. She couldn't wait to lose her next tooth.

Funny, isn't it?

Abby was so afraid to lose that first tooth. She did everything in her power to keep that old baby tooth in place. But when the tooth finally lost out to a lollipop, Abby was thrilled to see it go because of all the benefits that accompanied the monumental event.

Later, as I thought about Abby's loose-tooth experience, I realized that I had some "loose teeth" in my own life—things I was holding back from God—things I was afraid to let go of. I didn't want to give them to God. I was afraid to lose them.

If I give them to God, there will be gaping holes in my life, I thought. *I just can't let go of them.*

I imagine Abby was afraid to lose her tooth for the same reason. She probably feared she would have a toothless smile forever. Besides, her old tooth was so comfortable. She had grown used to it and was afraid she'd miss it.

I had held on to the "loose teeth" in my life for the same reasons.

But you know what? When I finally let loose of those things in my life, God replaced them with better, stronger, and more beautiful ones—just as Abby's beautiful, white permanent tooth replaced the old, weakened baby one.

Permanent teeth are a sign of maturity, both in the spiritual and the natural. I have a question for you: How are your spiritual teeth? If you resemble Snaggletooth, or if you're still walking around with a mouthful of worn-out baby teeth, it's time to let go and let God. It's time to join the "Lost Tooth Club" and enjoy the benefits of membership. Trust me, God gives a lot better rewards than that leopard-print slipper-wearing tooth fairy.

THOUGHT for the day: Do you have any "loose teeth" in your life? Are you afraid to let go of them?

SCRIPTURE reading: Matthew 6:24-34; 16:24-28; Mark 10:28-31.

DAILY declaration: Dear Lord, this very day, I give You all of the things in my life that I have been keeping from You. I am letting go and letting You replace those things with more of You. I thank You for loving me, and I thank You for helping me grow up in You.

Chapter Ten

IT'S OKAY,

mommy

Making Prayer
Instinctive

As I watered my fern on our front porch, I studied the front yard. We had just moved in two weeks before, and the former owners had neglected the yard for what appeared to be years.

There's so much work to do, I thought.

Our yard looked like a jungle, and not a lush, green, thriving jungle. In fact, our yard looked more like a jungle that had been through some sort of freak chemical spill, killing all of the grass and leaving only hideous weeds. It was a scary sight.

But we were determined to save it. The whole family decided to pitch in and make something of our yard. Jeff began trimming the overgrown hedges, and the girls and I started picking up debris and large sticks from the yard. After an hour or so, I retreated to the cool air-conditioning for a soda break. Moments later, Allyson, then four years old, came tearing into the house, screaming at the top of her lungs.

"It bit me! It bit me!" she screamed, holding the calf of her right leg.

"What bit you?" I asked, expecting to see a mosquito bite.

"I don't know but it hurt!" she cried.

I knelt down and inspected Ally's calf. I saw a red, raised bump, but nothing too terrible-looking.

"I think you're going to live," I teased. "Probably just a fire ant or a pesky mosquito."

As any mom would do, I put some bug-bite ointment on the red bump and kissed Ally on the head.

"That should make it feel better," I said.

Allyson wiped her tears on the bottom of her untucked shirt and decided to take a soda break, too. The crying had stopped and everything seemed all right. We went back outside and worked out in the yard until dusk before calling it a day.

While I was giving Allyson her bath that night, I noticed the red bump had become a little larger, but it didn't look alarming. So I put some more ointment on it and tucked her into bed. Daddy prayed with her and Abby, and we all retreated to our rooms for a good night's rest.

The next morning, I was awakened by the sunlight spilling in through our bedroom blinds.

It's going to be a beautiful day, I thought.

Then my eyes glanced at the alarm clock. It read, "7:35 A.M."

"7:35 A.M.! Oh no! Jeff, we overslept!" I said as I jumped out of bed.

I had twenty-five minutes to get dressed, get the girls ready, pack lunches, get them to school and me to work. It would take a major miracle.

The next half hour was a complete blur as we all rushed to get out the door on time. The girls dressed

and fed themselves while I threw on a pantsuit, brushed
my teeth, put my hair in a clip, and packed their lunches.
On the way out the door, I put their hair in ponytails,
and we piled into our SUV.

I dropped them off at school, drove like a madwoman
to work, and rushed inside my office at 8:32 A.M.—only
two minutes late.

Just as I plopped down into my office chair, the
phone rang.

Oh no, I thought. *My boss must've noticed I came in a
little late.*

"Hello," I said sheepishly.

"Mrs. Adams, I am calling about Allyson," I heard
the voice say on the other end of the line. "Have you
looked at her leg? She has a very serious bite of some
sort, and I think you need to take her to see a doctor."

My heart sank into my stomach. In all of the confu-
sion, I realized I hadn't even looked at the bite on her leg
that morning.

"You know, we were working in the yard yesterday,
and she said something had bitten her, but we didn't
know what," I explained.

"Mrs. Adams, it looks a lot like a wound from a
brown recluse spider. I don't say that to scare you, but I
think you need to get her to the doctor right now."

My mouth dropped open and I froze. I couldn't
believe what I was hearing. We had just moved to Texas,
so I wasn't up on all of the poisonous insects in the area,
but I had heard of the brown recluse spider, and I knew
its bite could be bad.

"I'll be right there," I said, hanging up.

Minutes later, I was at Ally's school, inspecting her leg. The bite was no longer red. It had turned dark, almost black in color, surrounded by a perfect circle of purplish-red. It was so swollen that it was visible beneath her pant leg.

I started to panic.

I called a nearby pediatrician from my cell phone, described Allyson's wound, and told the nurse that we were on our way. Then I called Jeff and my mother and blubbered a few minutes to each of them. All the while, Allyson sat quietly in the backseat. She was very calm.

That's probably the effect of the poison in her system, I reasoned. *She is probably going into some sort of shock.*

I sobbed even louder as I raced to the doctor's office.

Then I heard a sweet little voice from the backseat say, "It's okay, Mommy. I already prayed about my leg."

I looked at her in amazement through my rear-view mirror.

Allyson had peace because she had already given the situation to the Father. At age four, she knew the most important thing to do in a crisis—pray. I, at twenty-nine, had totally missed it.

Allyson remained calm throughout the hysterical outbursts of her mother, the poking and prodding of the doctor and nurses, the injection of medicine into her leg—all of it. She was a pillar of strength, and I was a quivering bowl of emotional jello.

I finally calmed down once I heard the doctor say, "She is going to be just fine. If she were going to take a turn for the worse, it would have already happened. Just watch the wound overnight and bring her back tomorrow for another shot."

I nodded, thanked the doctor, and hugged Allyson so hard she said, "Ouch."

Allyson's leg took a few weeks to heal, but eventually, all signs of the bite disappeared. However, memories of that spider bite will stick with me forever.

The whole episode taught me a very important lesson—go to God first.

Instinctively, Allyson prayed—before she did anything else. I, on the other hand, panicked, cried, called my family members and cried to them, and then panicked some more. Prayer was the last thing on my mind, when it should've been the first.

Even though I prayed over my children every day, I didn't think to run to God when the "spider-bite scare" happened. I tried to handle it myself, and when it seemed too big, I became overwhelmed with emotion.

As ashamed as I was about my lack of instinctive prayer, I was equally proud of Allyson's automatic prayer reaction. I had taught her well. I just needed a refresher course myself. So I enrolled in Holy Spirit 101 and got right with God concerning my prayer instincts.

How are your instincts? Do you try to handle everything yourself, or do you go to God in prayer immediately? Is He the first person you turn to, or do you get on the phone and look for answers and comfort from family and friends? Perhaps you, too, need a refresher course. If you do, come on into Holy Spirit 101. I'll save you a seat.

THOUGHT for the day: Go to God first. He has all the answers and comfort you need for any crisis you might be facing today.

SCRIPTURE reading: Matthew 6:25-34; Ephesians 6:10-18; 1 Peter 5:7.

DAILY declaration: Today, I choose to go to You, God, in all things. I realize that I can't handle them on my own. Father, I ask that You help me to make prayer instinctive in my life, and I thank You for performing that work in me right now. I love You, Lord.

Chapter Eleven

WHY'D WE
have to
move?

Going Through
Changes with God

I stared at the mound of boxes in my garage and wanted to burst into tears.

I will never get unpacked, I thought as I stood in the hot garage of our newly acquired Texas home.

It was our first big move. Jeff and I had lived in the same small southern Indiana town our entire lives. We met when I was an eighth-grader and he was a sophomore in high school. We were high school sweethearts, dating off and on for seven years, before marrying right after college.

In those seven years of marriage, we had moved into our first home in the same neighborhood where I'd grown up, had two children, become active in our home church, and worked in the community that had always been so good to us. (Did I mention that my parents lived next door?) Our roots ran very deep, so to make a major move was like uprooting a seventy-five-year-old oak tree. Moving meant tremendous upheaval in our lives, yet we knew we were doing the right thing. We knew in our hearts that God was leading us to Fort Worth, Texas—thousands of miles from our Hoosier home.

It was scary.

As I sorted through another box, placing spices in my kitchen cabinet, I could feel my heart pounding in my throat.

I hope we made the right decision, I thought.

I was an emotional mess, trying to maintain some sort of composure for the sake of Abby and Allyson, who were five and three at the time. They had been forced to move away from all their friends, their preschool, their grandparents, their playroom, and the swing set that Daddy had built them. Life as they'd always known it was now over. We were making a new start in a new city. They'd have to make new friends in a new school, and Abby wasn't handling the transition very well, though I hadn't noticed because I had been so wrapped up in my own mixed emotions.

Weeks later as I unpacked the last box, I sighed with relief. The house was actually coming together. I had started to like our new Texas home. It wasn't Indiana, but Texas had a lot of character that I was growing to love. I even went out and bought a pair of boots and a cowboy hat just so I'd feel a little more local.

As I carried the empty box to the roadside for trash pickup, I noticed Abby sitting on the curb, playing in a small mound of sand.

"How's it going, Ab?" I called.

"Terrible," she grumbled.

I walked over and plopped down right beside her.

"What seems to be the trouble?" I asked, trying to be upbeat.

"Everything."

"Anything I can do?"

"Yeah," she said, "you could move us back to Indiana."

That's when I realized that Abby wasn't adjusting as well as I'd hoped. Allyson was doing great, but she was a different temperament from Abby. Abby favored my disposition, whereas Allyson took after her daddy's easy-going manner. It was no wonder why Abby was having a more difficult time. The move had hurt her deeply and she was angry.

"I hate it here. Why'd we have to move? There's no park. We don't have a swing set, and I miss Mamaw and Papaw and Nana and Granddad."

"I know," I comforted, pulling her close to me. "I miss all of them, too."

"Why can't it be the way it used to be? I want my old life back!" Abby cried, pulling away and running into the house.

As I watched Abby in so much pain, my heart hurt for her. I knew some of what she was experiencing because I was going through the same emotions, but I didn't know exactly how she felt. After all, I'd been able to live in the same hometown for twenty-eight years. I had never had to transfer elementary schools, make new friends, or leave family members. But, at age six, we were asking her to do all of that, and she felt overwhelmed. She just couldn't understand how anything good could ever come of our move.

There were days when I wondered that myself, but I could see the big picture with the help of God's binoculars. Abby could only see one thing—her world was radically different—and she didn't like it one bit.

Isn't that how we sometimes act with God? We can only see the situation from one perspective—ours—and we don't like what we see, so we protest. We cry out to God, "Why'd I have to move? I want my old life back!"

I can think of so many times when I have been really angry with God for allowing circumstances to change in my life. There have been times when I've fought Him every step of the way when He tried to move me into new areas of growth.

Why? Because change is scary. It forces us out of our comfort zones, and many times it stretches us more than we want to be stretched. Think of the caterpillar. I bet he isn't too thrilled when he has to give up his freedom and hole up in a cramped cocoon for a long time. But after he goes into the cocoon, a marvelous transformation begins to take place, and the end result is wonderful. He gets to emerge a beautiful butterfly, free to fly in a bright new world, able to see everything from an entirely new perspective.

If that caterpillar didn't form that cocoon and undergo change, he'd never get to experience what it means to be a butterfly. If we don't let God work in us, change us, and move us into new places in life, we'll never get to fly either.

Yes, change is scary. Yes, it hurts. But God is able to carry us through change if only we'll let Him. The same way I hurt when I saw Abby in so much pain, God hurts when He sees us hurting. I wanted to make everything all right in Abby's world. I wanted to assure her that life would be grander in our new home, if she'd only hang on. God wants you to hang on, too. He wants to assure you that life will be even better where He is taking you, whether it be a physical, emotional, or spiritual move.

It's been a few years since our move, and I'm happy to report that Abby has adjusted quite nicely. She has a whole new set of friends. She loves her new school, and she's talked Daddy into building her another swing set.

We still have some "homesick days" when we long for colorful Indiana autumns, Indiana University basketball games at Assembly Hall, shopping trips to the College Mall in Bloomington, visits to Snow's Drive-In for Cherry colas and onion rings, and lazy Sunday afternoons at Nana and Granddad's house (my parents, "Mamaw and Papaw," moved here last year), but we've planted new roots in this Texas soil. We don't yet have a seventy-five-year-old oak tree, but we believe someday we'll be as grounded here as we were in Indiana.

The transition hasn't been easy, but God has been faithful to help us face each new challenge. So don't run from the moving van in your life. God has great plans for you. Quit asking, "Why'd I have to move?" and start praising Him for the butterfly you're about to become. Change is a good thing. Change is a God thing.

THOUGHT for the day: Are you resisting change in your life? Are you afraid of change? Remember the caterpillar. Why crawl when you can fly?

SCRIPTURE reading: Joshua 1:3, 9; Jeremiah 29:11; 2 Corinthians 5:17.

DAILY declaration: Father, I repent for resisting change in my life. I ask that You help me to be full of faith and not full of fear where change is concerned. I long to be a butterfly, so help me, Lord, to be brave enough to leave the comfort of my caterpillar world.

Chapter Twelve

how many
more days,
MOMMY?

Enjoying the
Presence of God

"Owww! Not so hard," Abby yelled as I brushed her hair into a perfect ponytail.

"There, all done," I said, looking at Abby in the bathroom mirror. "That will keep your hair off your neck so you won't be hot in gym class today."

"Can I wear my hair *down* when I go to Mandy's?" she asked.

"Sure, if you want."

"How many more days, Mommy?" Abby asked, her eyes dancing with enthusiasm.

Teasing, I asked, "How many more days until what?"

"Mommy," she whined. "How many more days until we go to Mandy's to spend the night?"

"Oh," I said, smiling. "Four more days from today."

"That's a long time," she said with a half-pout.

"It'll be here before you know it."

With that, my seven-year-old was off to collect her backpack and lunch box for school. It was Ally's turn in the "beauty shop."

"C'mon, Al!" I called. "Hurry! You don't want to be late for school."

Ally, my kindergartner, dragged into the bathroom as though she'd just discovered that Cartoon Network was going off the air.

"What's with the pouty face?" I asked, raking a comb through her blond curls.

"Abby told me," she mumbled.

"Abby told you what?"

"That it's four days away."

"Well, I should think you'd be excited about going to Mandy's," I said matter-of-factly while securing a red bow on top of her head.

"But that's too long. I want to go tonight," she said, almost in tears.

"Well, honey, you can't spend the night tonight. It's a school night," I explained. "You'll just have to wait until Friday."

Spending the night at Mandy's was the highlight of the season. On the list of "Kids Favorite Things to Do," going to Mandy's fell somewhere between going to McDonald's Playland and going fishing with Daddy. As Abby likes to say, "It's way fun."

Mandy, my twenty-three-year-old niece, was the epitome of cool to Abby and Ally. They loved everything about her—from her gorgeous auburn hair to her silver toe ring. Plus, Mandy made sure the girls had plenty of fun when they spent the night at her apartment.

They got to do all of the things I won't let them do at home, such as paint their own toenails with glittery nail polish, put makeup on each other, order pizza at midnight, and watch movies all night long.

No wonder Mandy was such a hit; even I wanted to go along. Of course, they wouldn't hear of that. Nope, going to Mandy's was their special time. They certainly didn't want their old mom tagging along—not on a night with their cool cousin.

As the week progressed, it was the same routine: "How many more days, Mommy?"

I must've heard that question ninety-two million times that week. By Wednesday the girls were bursting with anticipation of the big night. So I decided to use the situation to my advantage.

"Abby! Allyson!" I called from the kitchen.

I could hear the pitter-patter of little feet running down the hallway.

"Yes, Mother," they said in unison.

"I was thinking," I whispered in my this-is-supposed-to-get-you-really-excited-kind-of-voice. "If you clean up your playroom closet, I'll let you pack for Mandy's tonight."

And the crowd went wild! The girls cheered and jumped around just at the thought of packing their ever fashionable 101 Dalmatian suitcases.

"Okay," Abby said, dashing down the hall toward her playroom with Allyson two steps behind her.

More than an hour later, Abby announced that the playroom closet was ready for my inspection. As I peered into the playroom, I could not believe my eyes. They had actually stacked, sorted, picked up, put away, and organized the dreaded playroom closet. I was duly impressed.

So the packing commenced.

The girls chose every item with great care as they filled up their tiny suitcases. They debated over which movies to take, asking each other, "Which one do you

think Mandy will like best?" They tried on several night-
ies to see which would be the perfect one to wear at
Mandy's, and they thoughtfully chose the best stuffed
animal to take along on their Night O' Fun.

When the suitcases were finally packed, we placed
them in the back of our SUV—two whole days before
we'd need them. But that made the girls happy, so it was
fine with me.

As the alarm blared in my ears on Friday morning, I
awoke to find two little girls hovering over me.

"How long have you been up?" I groaned, trying to
open one eye.

"A long time," Abby said. "We already got dressed.
You need to do our hair."

I reached across the bed to make sure Jeff was awake
before stumbling into the bathroom to plug in the hot
rollers and curling iron.

An hour later we were off. It was another weekday
morning, but not just *any* weekday morning—it was
Friday. And it wasn't just *any* Friday. It was "going-to-
Mandy's" Friday, and the natives were extremely restless.

They both had a certain spring in their step that
morning. Abby didn't say, "Owww!" one time as I
brushed the tangles from her hair. And Allyson didn't
even mind that I had used grape jelly instead of her
favorite apple jelly when making her lunch.

Life was good.

When I went to pick them up after school, I could
see that the happiness had continued throughout the day.
I smiled as I watched Abby and Allyson skipping out of

school, holding hands. They bounded over and piled
into the backseat. Abby did a quick inspection, making
sure the suitcases were still in the very back, and then
buckled her seatbelt.

"It's time, isn't it, Mommy?" Allyson asked.

"Yep," I answered. "I'm taking you to Mandy's
right now."

On the thirty-minute trip to Mandy's, the girls
giggled and sang along with the radio. There was so
much "Zip-A-Dee-Doo-Dah" in the air, I wouldn't have
been surprised to see a cartoon bluebird land on my
shoulder. The girls were full of anticipation, happiness,
excitement, and lots of giggles.

When I pulled up in front of Mandy's apartment,
Abby squealed, "We're here! We're here!"

I barely parked the car before the girls were banging
on Mandy's door. As soon as she opened the door, the
fun commenced. They tackled her in the doorway, and
the Night O' Fun was off to a great start. I brought in
the suitcases, kissed the girls, thanked Mandy, and
headed home.

On the drive home, I couldn't help but smile, just
thinking about how excited the girls were to be with
Mandy. They loved her that much. They would have
done anything to be with her—even clean up their playroom closet. As I thought about them, my mind turned
to spiritual matters. I thought, *Wouldn't it be great if they
were that excited when Sunday morning rolled around, and
they had looked forward all week long to attending church?*

Usually, they moaned and groaned about having to get up and get ready to go to church.

"It's boring and you don't get good snacks there," Allyson informed me every Sunday morning.

I couldn't fault my girls for their lack of enthusiasm because I wasn't exactly excited about attending church either. Oh, I liked church, but I certainly didn't anticipate each service. No, it was more of a "have to" thing for me. I hadn't always felt that way, but somewhere along the way, my heart had stopped longing to be in God's house the way it once had.

I wasn't exactly waiting with bated breath to have my daily devotion time with God either. Had I grown cold to the things of God? I was afraid to answer that question. I still loved God. I still wanted to serve Him with my whole heart, but I wasn't too excited about being with Him anymore.

I realized on that drive home from Mandy's that I had developed a heart attitude problem. And it was a contagious heart problem that was being reflected in my children's attitude toward God.

All of the "Zip-A-Dee-Doo-Dah" had zipped right out of the vehicle, but I was grateful the Holy Spirit had pointed out the issue so that I could do something about it. And that's exactly what I did.

I repented for allowing my heart to grow cold toward God, and I began to thank Him for all of His wondrous works in my life. As I praised Him, I could feel my heart rejoicing in a way I hadn't felt in a while. I asked the Lord to restore that longing in my heart for

Him, and I thanked Him for loving me enough to want me in His presence.

A tremendous change took place in me that day. My attitude changed. I regained the same excitement that had been there when I first gave my heart to Jesus. Yes, I still have to get "Holy Spirit booster shots" to keep my heart problem from returning, but the more I consistently walk with God, the more I *want* to walk with Him.

Now, just as Abby and Allyson long to spend time with their cool cousin, I long to spend time with my Creator. He shows me insights in His Word. He gives me witty ideas when we're together. He lets me talk about my day, and He loves me as nobody else can. Our times together just keep getting better and better!

So if your heart has grown cold to the things of God, there is hope. God doesn't hold grudges. He will help you fix your heart problem, and before you know it, you'll be enjoying His presence again. And the best part is you don't have to wait until Friday. You can be with Him right now!

THOUGHT for the day: Has your heart grown cold to the things of God? Do you look forward to spending time with Him?

SCRIPTURE reading: Psalms 9:1-2; 106: 1-2; 2 Corinthians 6:16b-18.

DAILY declaration: Dear Lord, today I repent for losing that passion that I once had for You, and I ask that You renew my heart so that it longs for more of You. I love You, Lord, and I praise You for who You are. I'm looking forward to spending quality time together—just You and me. Amen.

Chapter Thirteen

I THOUGHT
you loved
me!

Learning to Love
God's Discipline

As I sorted through Monday's mail, I put the various envelopes in piles of priority: bills, correspondence from friends and family, magazines and catalogs, junk mail, and all other pieces of mail.

On this particular day, the "all other pieces of mail" pile contained a letter for Abby. She was becoming quite the first-grade socialite in her new school. It seemed that every week she was invited to a sleepover or a birthday party. No doubt, this was another invitation.

"Abby," I called. "There's a letter for you."

Sounding like a herd of elephants, Abby, Allyson, and the family dogs came thundering into the kitchen.

"Where is it?" Abby asked, scanning the mail piles.

"Right on top, the pink one," I said, motioning to the correct pile.

Abby ripped open the envelope with much enthusiasm.

"It's from Rachel," she said. "Can I go to her birthday party, *please*?"

"Probably," I answered, reading the invitation for myself: a birthday party for Rachel at Chuck E. Cheese's on Saturday at 3 P.M.

"That sounds like fun, Ab," I encouraged. "We'll have to buy her a present one night this week."

"Can we go tonight?"

"Might as well," I said. "If we're going to go tonight, let's do it now."

With that, we all loaded into the SUV and headed to the local Wal-Mart. Once inside "Wally World," the girls rushed to the toy section. It was as if a massive magnet pulled them in that direction. They were on a mission: a toy-buying mission. The problem was, this toy buying was for someone else, not exactly Abby and Ally's favorite kind of assignment. This had put them in an irritable mood.

Aisle after aisle, the girls inspected dolls, games, stuffed animals, yo-yos, puzzles, squirt guns, dress-up clothes, and every other kind of toy imaginable. As I tried to figure out how to work one of the latest computer games, my concentration was broken by a loud squeal.

"Stop it, Abby!"

"I don't have to, stupid!"

"I'm not stupid, you idiot! I'm telling. *Mom!*"

My first thought was, *Do I ignore them and act as though they are someone else's children?*

As the fighting intensified, I decided to swallow my pride in front of the other parents roaming the toy aisles and deal with World War III.

By the time I made it to the feuding sisters, Abby had shoved Allyson into a display of stuffed toys and sent them flying in every direction.

"Stop it right now!" I said through gritted teeth and squinted eyes. "What do you think you're doing?"

"She started it," Abby said.

"Did not," Ally said between gasps and sobs.

"Well, I don't care who started it. You're both grounded," I said, using my mom-logic, passed on to me from my mother. "I'll not tolerate this behavior—not now, not ever!"

I took each of them by the hand and dragged them out of the store, past the mass of people, through the parking lot, and finally into our vehicle.

No one said a word the entire drive home. I was too mad to "parent" at that time, and the girls were too afraid to even dare plead their cases. As soon as we pulled into the driveway, I voiced the verdict: "Allyson, you're grounded from TV for the rest of the week. Abby, you're grounded from going to Rachel's party."

"But, *Mom!*" they whined in unison.

"No, I don't want to hear any whining. Just go to your rooms," I snapped.

I was tired and frustrated, and my feet were aching. I was so relieved when Jeff came home moments later. I relayed the story to him and asked him to talk to his children about using the words "stupid" and "idiot," and about shoving each other, and about anything else he wanted to throw in for good measure.

Seeing I was spent, Jeff obliged while I watched some mindless reruns on TV.

Throughout the rest of the week, the girls tried to make up for their in-store outburst. In fact, they were almost perfect. They kept their rooms picked up without me having to prod them. They did their homework without me reminding them. They brushed their teeth without a fight. They even went to bed without much of a fuss.

It was almost scary. I was sure the invasion of the body snatchers had happened, leaving me with pod peewees in place of Abby and Ally.

By Friday afternoon, I was feeling rather lenient and forgiving. I thought, *I'll give them a break and lift their punishment starting today.*

When I announced my merciful decision, Abby jumped up and down with excitement, while Allyson ran to the TV to catch the last few minutes of a favorite cartoon.

I felt like less of an ogre and more of a mother while I was preparing dinner that evening. All was well with the world, until Allyson borrowed Abby's gel pens. Then the situation turned ugly really fast.

The next thing I knew, Allyson came running into the kitchen with a large red mark on her arm where Abby had punched her. Of course, Allyson had it coming. She knew better than to get into Abby's things, but there was no excuse for violence. So I was left with no other choice than to reinstate the original discipline.

"Abby, get in here right now!" I hollered.

Sheepishly, Abby wandered into the kitchen. Allyson turned up her crying a notch, which added to the drama of the moment.

"You guys blew it," I said. "This last episode has left me no choice but to re-ground you. So no TV, Allyson, and no party for you, Abby."

"But, *Mom!*" Abby said. "I have to go. I already called Rachel and told her I was coming."

"Well, you'll just have to call her back and tell her that you can't make it because you are being disciplined for fighting with your sister."

Tears welled up in Abby's big green eyes. "But, Mom," she whimpered. "I thought you loved me."

A wave of guilt tried to overtake me.

"I do love you, Abby, and that's why I can't let you get away with this bad behavior. I discipline and guide you *because* I love you. If I didn't care, I'd just let you act any way you wanted, but I love you enough to enforce healthy boundaries when you act the way you did today," I explained. "Do you understand?"

"*No!*" she screamed. "You just don't love me."

Then she ran to her room to pout the night away.

As they say in Texas, I felt lower than a snake's belly. I wanted to let her go to the party. I knew it meant a lot to her, but I'd already given her a chance to redeem herself, and she'd blown it. I couldn't budge on this one. Letting her go was the easy way out, and I knew that wasn't in her best interest. She needed to learn that her actions had repercussions.

When 3 P.M. rolled around on Saturday, Abby cried genuine tears. She wanted to be at the pizza place with all her friends and the big, loud mouse that dances and annoys all the parents. But, instead, she was at home with Allyson, Daddy, and me.

I knelt down and wiped Ab's tears. Like any parent, I wanted to hug away her hurt because I hurt for her. I wanted to let her go, but I knew I couldn't. As I struggled with my decision, I wondered if that's how God feels every time He has to correct me? The more I thought about it, the more I realized that's exactly how God feels when He corrects His children.

He hurts for us. He wants us to enjoy all the good things He has created for us—He want to bless us. He wants the best for our lives. When we disobey, He seeks our repentance and lovingly guides us toward obedience.

As I pondered this realization, I began studying about the children of Israel—God's chosen people. God was good to them. He heard their cries when they were being mistreated in Egypt, and He answered them. By miraculous signs and wonders, He delivered them from their lives of slavery and misery. He took them out of captivity and promised them a land that flowed with milk and honey. He longed to take them to the Promised Land, but they kept disobeying His commandments.

Time and time again, they acted in rebellion against Almighty God. They complained when He fed them manna from Heaven because they had become discontented. They talked against God's chosen leader, Moses, and ultimately against God, saying, "Why did you bring us out of Egypt into this desert to die?" Then they became impatient with God, waiting for His instruction, and they built a golden idol to worship. Talk about disobedience.

God, in His mercy, gave them many chances, but they continued to sin against Him. What should have been an eleven-day trip took them forty years. They wandered in the wilderness of disobedience instead of dwelling in the Promised Land. Finally, because of their continued disobedience not one person from that generation entered into the Promised Land, except for Caleb and Joshua who were rewarded for following the Lord wholeheartedly.

As I meditated this, I felt somewhat closer to God. I felt as if I knew Him more, as if I knew His heart better than I'd ever known it before. I could clearly see the love He has for all of His children, and how much it hurts Him when we walk in disobedience.

I could almost imagine Him cringing each time I took a detour from obedience, calling to me, "Hey, Michelle. Don't do that. I can't bless you if you go that way. C'mon now, go this way instead. I love you. I want the best for you."

And when I flat-out rebelled and ignored His voice, I could imagine Him sighing with Fatherly disappointment, saying, "Please don't walk in the wilderness. I love you, but I can't bless you until you come to a place of repentance. I'll be here waiting for you, loving you, and longing to bless you."

If you've been wandering in the wilderness for a while, isn't it time to get right with God and enter into the blessings He has in store for your life? He's been waiting for you. It's not too late. His arms are open wide, and He's ready to hug away your hurt and put you back on the right road. And you know what? You can expect a life full of wonderful blessings and fellowship with the

Father—even better than pizza parties with a dancing mouse. Imagine that.

THOUGHT for the day: Are you walking in the land of disobedience and missing out on the Promised Land that God has for you?

SCRIPTURE reading: Numbers 14; Hebrews 12:6-11.

DAILY declaration: Father God, I ask that You would help me be sensitive to Your leading and that I would quickly come to a place of repentance when I have been in a posture of disobedience. Thank You for loving me enough to guide and direct my way so that I might grow up in You and walk in the fullness of Your blessings. Amen.

Chapter Fourteen

WATCH

me, mom!

Understanding That God's Approval
Is All You Need

The birds were singing. The sun was shining. The flowers were blooming. Yes, spring fever had filled the air at the Adams' household, and Abby and Allyson were beyond stir crazy. They could hardly wait to get outside and play.

During each dreary day of winter, the girls had dreamed of catching roly-poly bugs, chasing butterflies, riding bicycles, flying kites, driving Barbie Jeeps, making mud pies, and, more than anything else, going to the park.

Ahhh, the park.

The park, to my seven- and five-year-old, was the ultimate in fun. And since the park was only a few minutes away, I decided to make it a fun Mommy day by picnicking at the park.

I loaded up lots of snacks, drinks, napkins, a blanket, sunglasses, and a good romance novel (the same one I'd been trying to finish for the past eight months), and we headed that way.

Upon arrival, we could see that apparently everyone in the city of Fort Worth was suffering from the same spring fever. The park was packed with people, but the girls didn't mind. They dashed to the nearest set of monkey bars and began climbing to the top while I plopped down at a nearby picnic table, opened my book, and began reading. After a few moments, I was back into the story.

How could I have put this down without finishing it? I wondered as I became entranced in the story of Frank and Hannah.

Hannah and Frank were in the middle of a lovers' spat, and just as it was getting good, I heard, "Mom! Mom!"

Pulled back into reality, I placed the book on the table and followed the voice with my eyes. It was Abby.

"Watch me, Mom!" she called as she swung upside down like a monkey.

"That's good, Ab. Be careful, though."

I gave Abby the "thumbs up sign," picked up my book, and drifted back to the fight scene. Back and forth they argued, but Frank couldn't stay mad at Hannah for long. He loved her too much. Just then, she slammed the door and broke a dish.

"Mom! Mom! Watch me, Mom!"

Snapped back to present day, I again looked up to see Abby sliding down a fireman's pole. Smiling her tooth-less grin, she giggled as she sped down the pole.

"That's neat," I said, smiling back at her.

After a quick scan to locate Allyson, I returned to the story.

> *Frank studied her again. So that was what this was all about. She'd gone just a little further than*

*she'd wanted in this expression of opposition and had
come to him to find a way of calling a truce.*

*Leaning against the closed door, Frank grinned
and held out his arms for her to come to him.*[1]

"Mom! Watch me, Mom!"

Slowly, I lifted my eyes from the page and focused on
Abby, standing at the top, near the edge of the big, curvy
slide. The gentle breeze blew her brown pigtails behind
her as she prepared to conquer the slide. She glanced my
way to make sure I was watching before gliding down
the slide.

It was obvious...Frank and Hannah would have to
wait. I wasn't going to get any reading done because I
had a more important job to do. My job was to watch,
smile, clap, and give the "thumbs up sign," showing my
approval for the many playground performances taking
place all around me.

For the next two hours, I watched Abby and Allyson
climb, swing, slide, jump, run, and skip. Each time, Abby
(more than Allyson) would make sure my attention was
focused on her before attempting a new daring feat.

Later, the girls joined me for a picnic. We munched
peanut butter and jelly sandwiches and crunched potato
chips as the afternoon sun gave way to the evening. As I
loaded everything into our vehicle, I reflected on the day.
It had been so much fun, probably the most fun we'd
had together in months.

It wasn't what I had planned for the afternoon. I
wanted to lose myself in a Christian romance novel, but

the girls wanted me to lose myself in them. More than I realized, they needed my approval. They longed for my praise. And it thrilled me to offer that affirmation to them. I was a natural-born cheerleader, so I played that role well when it came to my children.

As I thought about my cheerleading role, I realized that God often plays that same role in my life. So many times, I call to Him, "Watch me, God!" because I long for His approval. I want Him to be proud of me, just as Abby longs for me to be proud of her.

There have been times in my life when I've taken the less-traveled road, the road that many of my friends and family sometimes didn't understand or even agree with. Yet, I knew I was following God's leading. It's at those times when I've called out to God, "Watch me, God!" hoping for His affirmation because no one else seemed to offer any. He has always come through with a "thumbs up" or an encouraging word.

Though most who know me would assume I am very self-confident and sure of myself, I'm usually not. So many times I stand on the edge of a decision the same way Abby stood at the edge of the slide. I glance in God's direction, just to make sure He's watching me. Knowing He has His eye on me somehow gives me the confidence to press forward and go with that inward leading.

Then, when it's all said and done, and I've come through a tough time or I've accomplished a goal, I look in His direction again. I never find His nose shoved in a book. No, He is always watching me, cheering me on, making me feel so special.

When I think of God, I don't think of some rigid, all-powerful being with a big club in hand, ready to whop me on the head whenever I make a mistake. No, when I think of God, I see a loving Heavenly Father with a smile on His face, cheering me on to victory. Whether I'm on the monkey bars of life or standing on the edge of a big, curvy slide, God's eyes are always on me. Somehow, that makes every disappointment easier and every victory sweeter.

Maybe you don't have anyone in your life who gives you words of praise or the affirmation that you desire. Maybe you struggle with self-confidence, too, always longing for someone's approval. Or maybe you've been so discouraged in life that you're afraid to even climb the steps of the ladder that lead to the big, curvy slide. If you fit in any of those categories, it's okay, because God wants to fill that void in your life. He has enough love and affirmation to go around. He's been watching you all along. You just haven't looked in His direction for a while. So why don't you take a moment and look to God today? He has a "thumbs up" reserved just for you.

THOUGHT for the day: Do you long for God's approval? You've already got it if you're a child of the King. Look to Him today.

SCRIPTURE reading: Psalms 33:12-15; 139:1-18; 1 Peter 3:12.

DAILY declaration: Heavenly Father, thank You for loving me so much. I am so glad, Lord, that Your eyes are always on me, and that You are in my corner, cheering me on to victorious living. I appreciate You, Lord.

Chapter Fifteen

MILLER

did it!

Playing the Blame Game
Never Produces Winners

It was a typical evening at the Adams' household. My husband, Jeff, had plopped down on the bed and was busy paying bills. Abby, who was six at the time, was pretending to practice her spelling words while actually watching cartoons. And Allyson, who was four, was playing with Miller, our newly acquired dashing dachshund and her newest best buddy. I, on the other hand, was frantically searching the house for our only pair of scissors that never seem to be in the last place I left them.

"Jeff, have you seen the scissors?" I called from the kitchen.

"No, haven't seen them," he muttered.

"Well, I can't wrap this present for Linda's shower without scissors. The shower starts in twenty minutes! Could you help me look?" I begged.

The search began.

Not in the kitchen junk drawers. Not in the buffet junk drawer. Not in the medicine cabinet. Not in the mail basket.

"Any luck?" I called to Jeff.

"Nope," he hollered back.

Where could they be? I wondered.

Then it hit me. They could be in the pantry. I had used them earlier that day to cut open a bag of dog treats.

I bet I left them in there, I thought.

Quickly, I flung open the pantry door, fully expecting to find the scissors, but I found something else instead— a big, blond clump of hair sticking out of the trash can.

Oh no! Please let that hair be from one of the girls' dolls.

I picked up the hair and immediately identified it as Allyson's ponytail.

"Jeff!" I hollered. "You're not going to believe this."

Still holding the detached blond ponytail, I hurried to show him the evidence. Jeff peered over the top of the bills and focused in on the long blond hair in my hand.

"*Allyson!*" we said in unison.

The search began again—this time for the scissors and a four-year-old beautician.

Not in the playroom. Not in her bedroom. Not in her sister's room. Not in the bathroom.

"Allyson Michelle Adams!" I called as I charged down the hallway toward the laundry room, otherwise known as "the dachshund den."

The laundry room door slowly creaked open, and I heard a little voice say, "Yes, Mommy."

Jeff, who was right behind me, reminded me to stay calm.

I pushed open the door and stared at Allyson's head, horrified by what I saw. She had not only cut off her ponytail, but she had also cut a big portion of her bangs down to the scalp. It was a scary sight, especially since preschool pictures were the following Monday.

The look on my face must have spoken volumes because Allyson began to cry uncontrollably while Jeff began to laugh uncontrollably.

Jeff went back to paying bills, leaving me to deal with "Edward Scissorhands."

"Allyson, what's this?" I asked, showing her the pony-tail in my hand.

She dropped her head, avoiding eye contact with me.

"Did you cut your hair?" I accused.

"No," she answered.

"Then how did your hair end up like that?" I asked.

Allyson bit her lower lip, thought a minute, and then proudly declared, "Miller did it."

Upon hearing his name, Miller's tail began to beat against the nearby laundry basket.

Although Allyson's hair did look as if a dog had chewed it in various spots, I was pretty sure however, that Miller wasn't a clever enough canine to manipulate a pair of scissors. Thus, she had lied to me to cover her mistake.

I knelt beside Allyson, making eye contact with her, and said, "Now we have a big problem. You see, you've disobeyed Mommy and Daddy two times tonight. First, you used the scissors, which you know are off limits to you, and cut your hair, and then you lied about it and blamed it on poor Miller boy."

Again, the tail thuds commenced.

"The Bible says to 'honor your father and mother,' and it also says 'do not lie.' Al, I love you, but I don't love what you did."

"I'm sorry, Mommy!" she wept. "I'll never do it again. I promise!"

Allyson dropped to the floor and hid her face in Miller's black fur.

She cried. He wagged. And I tried to figure out what hat Allyson could wear for Monday's class picture.

Needless to say, I missed Linda's shower. I was so wound up from the whole hair ordeal that I decided to use my extra energy constructively. I decided to clean like a mad woman.

I began in Allyson's room.

As I stripped her bed, I found more hair. It was hidden under her pillow. When I vacuumed her carpet, I found clumps of hair behind the rocking chair. As I picked up her toys, I discovered still more strands sticking out from a book. She had hidden hair all over her room! She'd been quite creative in hiding the evidence.

Later, after I'd cleaned the entire house and put the kids to bed, I sunk into the sofa and pondered on what had happened that day. It was in those moments that the Lord dealt with me. I began to think about how many times I had blamed others for my past mistakes, the same way Allyson had blamed poor Miller. Then, just like Allyson, I had tried to hide the evidence of my wrongdoing, covering it up, hoping God wouldn't notice too much.

As God gently brought various incidents to my memory, I repented for each one. I went to bed that night promising I'd never do it again, just as Allyson had promised me.

Over the next few months as I watched Allyson's hair transform from a chewed-up mess to a mass of blond curls, it was a constant reminder of my promise to the Lord.

Will I ever mess up again? Probably, because I'm human. Will Allyson ever cut her hair again? I hope not, but even if she does get scissor-happy again, I'll still love her. And I'll still be there to comfort her and clean up her messes. Why? Because I love her more than life itself.

That's exactly how the Lord feels about us. He loves us more than we can comprehend. That's why He's so merciful with us. Even when we play the blame game and make messes in our lives, He forgives us, cleans up our messes, and restores us. Why? Because He loves us more than life itself. In fact, He gave His life for us.

Is there sin in your life that you've been blaming on someone else? If so, now is the perfect opportunity to confess it before the Lord and ask Him to forgive you. Soon you'll see that situation turn around, and just like Allyson, you'll be able to ditch the hat you've been hiding under and reveal the beautiful restoration that God has worked in your life.

THOUGHT for the day: Have you been playing the blame game? Do you need to ask God to forgive you?

SCRIPTURE reading: Romans 8:1-14; Ephesians 4:17-5:2.

DAILY declaration: Father, I am asking You to bring to my remembrance all of the times that I have blamed others for my wrongdoing. Right now, Father, I repent for those times and ask that You help me to walk in integrity. I ask that You help me to walk in Your ways all the days of my life. Amen.

Chapter Sixteen

WILL YOU
rock me?

Allowing God
to Love You

"Twenty minus nine," Abby mumbled, tapping her pencil against the kitchen table.

"Eleven," I volunteered while putting away the dinner dishes.

"Mom," Abby whined. "Don't help. I can do it myself."

"Sorry," I said.

I was getting used to that response. At age seven, Abby's favorite expression was, "I can do it myself. I'm not a baby!" As much as it hurt me to hear those words, it was true. She was no longer a baby. She was a twenty-five-year-old trapped in the body of a first-grader.

She was growing up into quite the little woman. She dressed herself. She enjoyed styling her own hair. She could fix herself meals that didn't require the oven. She earned her own money by doing chores. She put away her own laundry. She was a very independent little woman.

In fact, when we went shopping together, it was more like going with a gal pal than my little girl. She was growing up in every area of her life, and I didn't like it. I wanted to turn back the hands of time and keep her in that little-girl stage forever. But since that wasn't possible, I was bravely trying to let her mature and

experience the "I can do it myself" life without hinder-
ing her independence.

"C'mon, Abby," I called, waiting for her at the door.
"You're going to be late for your party."

Abby hurried to the door, wearing the third or fourth
outfit I'd seen her in that afternoon—a heart T-shirt and
a pair of designer blue jeans.

"Ready?" I quipped.

"Uh huh."

It was a Valentine's Day party at Molly's house, and
according to Abby, "Everyone was going to be there."

"Did you get your present for Molly?" I asked as we
loaded into the SUV.

"Yep," she said. "I even wrapped it myself."

I smiled at her in the rearview mirror as we made
our way to the party. After a few minutes of driving up
and down streets that all looked alike to me, I realized
that I was lost. I hadn't the foggiest idea where Molly
lived, and the directions on the invitation weren't
helping me either. I pulled over to the side of the road
and once again studied the little map that had come
with the invitation.

"It has to be right up here, but we've already been up
that way, and there is no corresponding house number to
Molly's," I said to myself. "I guess we'll look again."

"Mom, I bet it's one street over," Abby said, studying
the map.

She seemed confident, and I was out of ideas, so I
took Ab's advice. Sure enough, Molly's house was one

street over at the bottom of the hill. Abby had located it, reading the map much better than her dear old mom.

I dropped off Abby and headed into town to run a few errands.

"Now, don't be late," Abby coached. "I can't stay too long because I still have homework to do. This is a school night, you know."

"Okay," I said, waving good-bye.

Two hours later, I returned to Molly's to pick up Abby. After climbing into the front seat, Abby gave me the play-by-play party rundown.

It was some shindig.

Arts and crafts, popcorn balls, chocolate, games, dancing—a real blast.

When we arrived home, we discovered Daddy, Allyson, and the two dogs asleep in the den. We shut the door so we wouldn't disturb them, and then we plopped down in the living room—just Ab and me. I relaxed in the recliner, watching TV while Abby finished writing her spelling words three times each. She wrote her last word just as *The Brady Bunch* ended and *I Love Lucy* came on.

"Time for bed," I said. "Make sure you brush your teeth."

"Okay," she said. "I already laid out my clothes for tomorrow, but I need you to iron my shirt."

Minutes later, Abby returned to kiss me good-night. After a quick peck on the cheek, she wandered partway down the hall and then came back.

"What's wrong, honey?" I asked, noticing she had a perplexed look on her face.

"Nothin'."

"I'll iron your shirt in a little while," I said, thinking that was the problem.

"That's not it," Abby said.

"Well, what is it?" I asked.

"Nothin'."

"Then you better get to bed. It's getting late."

Abby gave me a hug, and then she looked up at me with her big green eyes and whispered, "Mama, will you rock me?"

So that's why she's been acting so funny, I thought. It was hard for my little grown-up girl to admit she wanted her mom to rock her. I'm sure, in her mind, big girls didn't need to be rocked. Still, she found the courage to ask.

Her request brought tears to my eyes. My big girl was asking me to rock her as I had so many nights when she was a baby. Nothing she could've asked me would have made me any happier.

I scooped up her long body and cuddled her on my lap as we watched Lucy and Ethel concoct one of their hair-brained schemes.

Ab fell asleep in my arms and I clung to her, wishing the moment would never end. I loved her more at that moment than I had ever loved her. I felt so close to her. Looking down at her as she slept, I thought about how much the Father loves us, His precious children.

You know, after we've been Christians for a while, we tend to get very independent and self-sufficient. I know there have been times in my life when I've taken matters into my own hands and said, "I can do it myself, Father. I'm not a baby."

I try to handle crises, make decisions, and live my life all on my own. Like Abby, I long to "do it myself," and God allows me my independence—even if it means letting me give the wrong answer to "twenty minus nine" sometimes. He loves me enough to let me figure things out on my own.

He also loves it when we swallow our pride, crawl up in His lap, and whisper, "Father, will You rock me?" It thrills Him as much as it thrilled me when Abby asked me that question.

God is our Father, and He enjoys loving His children. It blesses Him to scoop us up in His lap and cuddle us. It says in the Bible that we can come boldly into His throne room. Do you know why? Because He is our Dad, and what kind of Father would deny His children access to Him? He wants to be with us, nurture us, and love us. He gave His Son Jesus to die on the cross so that we could be in fellowship with Him for eternity. Now that's love.

So why not take advantage of your rights as a covenant child of God? Go ahead. Crawl up in His lap today and let Him love you awhile. He's got a recliner in the throne room, and His lap is always available to you.

THOUGHT for the day: Do you need a special touch from God today? Are you always trying to do everything on your own? Why don't you swallow your pride, crawl up in His lap, and let Him love you today? He's waiting.

SCRIPTURE reading: Luke 15:11-32; John 3:16; Hebrews 4:16; 1 John 4:16-19.

DAILY declaration: Heavenly Father, thank You for loving me even when I act independently of You. Thank You for understanding me. Lord, I need You today. I never want to be too proud to ask for Your help. Help me in this area. I want You to know that it means a lot to me, just knowing that I can crawl up in Your lap and spend time in Your presence. You are an awesome God and a precious Father. Amen.

Chapter Seventeen

WHICH

shoe goes
on which
foot?

Growing Up
in Jesus

J ust as we were rushing out the door on one of those marathon mornings, I realized that Allyson was still carrying around her tennis shoes.

"Why aren't your shoes on your feet?" I asked, halfway annoyed.

"Because," she whined, "you didn't tell me."

"Didn't tell you what?" I asked, bending down to help her with her shoes.

"You didn't tell me which shoe goes on which foot!" she said, tears in her eyes.

"Oh," I said. "Well, remember what Daddy told you? You match the curve of the shoe with the curve of your foot. That's how you tell which shoe goes on which foot."

She nodded as if she understood. I felt we'd made some sort of breakthrough, although the girls were sure to be late for school.

Oh well, I rationalized. *I'll just tell the tardy-pass lady that I was doing a little homeschooling this morning. Maybe she'll give us a break.*

No such luck. With tardy passes in hand, the girls wandered down the empty hallways to their classrooms. But at least Allyson's shoes were on the right feet, so that was a plus.

After school I decided to do something special for the girls, something to make up for such a crummy start to their day. As they loaded into the SUV, I said in my most excited Mom voice, "Do you girls want hamburgers for dinner?"

Cheers rang out from the ranks. The idea was a hit, so we headed off for the golden arches. I was kind of excited, too. It gave me an excuse to get a juicy cheeseburger. Yummy!

After wolfing down their kids meals, the girls slipped off their shoes, ran to the playland area, and disappeared inside the brightly colored tunnels. I finished my cheeseburger and read the newspaper to catch up on what was going on in the world beyond elementary school and cartoons. Just as I finished the sports section, my cell phone rang. It was my husband, Jeff. He had tracked me down. Now I had to confess—I had eaten a big cheeseburger, fries, and a large soft drink! Tae-Bo was calling my name.

"Okay, see ya soon," I said, hanging up.

It was time to go. Daddy would be home soon, and there was homework to do and baths to take. I motioned several times for Abby and Allyson, but they completely ignored me. So I decided to take another approach— bribery.

"*Abby* and *Allyson*!" I called to the little faces looking at me from a window in one of the tunnels. "C'mon. If you come right now, we'll still have time to get ice cream."

Those were the magic words. Down they came. First Abby, then Allyson.

Abby slipped on her sandals, took my money, and hurried to get her ice cream. Allyson, on the other hand, took her own sweet time, straightening her socks and untying her tennis shoes. She studied those shoes for several minutes. First she'd take a shoe and hold it up next to her foot, checking the curves to see if they matched. Then she'd take the other shoe and do the same. (I acted as though I was still reading the newspaper so I wouldn't add any extra pressure to the sticky situation.)

Finally, in total frustration, Allyson cried, "Which shoe goes on which foot?"

"Which shoe do you think goes on which foot?" I asked.

"I don't know," she said. "I just can't tell."

"Did you match the curves?"

"Yes, and it didn't help."

"Keep trying," I coached. "You can do it."

But Allyson was sick of trying to figure out which shoe went on which foot. She wanted her ice cream and she wanted it now, so she carried her shoes over to the food line and waited with her sister. I sighed a big sigh, realizing we hadn't experienced the monumental break-through that morning as I thought we had.

Oh well, I thought, *she'll get it in time.*

Once we were home, I made Jeff a grilled cheese sandwich (not nearly as yummy as my cheeseburger) while Abby finished copying her spelling words and Allyson finished her math worksheet.

With homework accomplished, bath time began. It was more like one of those automatic car washes that night. I ran them through the shower very quickly, slapped on some lavender lotion, dried their hair, and hurried them off to put on their pajamas.

After Daddy prayed with them, the girls came to me, bearing good-night kisses.

"G'night, Mommy," Abby said, planting one right on my cheek.

"'Night, kiddo."

"'Night, Mom. Love you," Allyson said, giving me a hug and a kiss.

As I gave her a hug in return, I glanced down at her bunny slippers. Their ears were pointing the wrong way, meaning just one thing. Allyson hadn't yet figured out which one went on which foot.

I didn't say a word. I just smiled and hugged her even more.

As Christians, we're a lot like that as we grow up in the Lord. There are many days when I can't figure out "which one goes on which foot" in so many areas of my life. I'll look at the situation, and like Allyson, I'll try to match it with the right solution. Sometimes I'll study that situation for hours, days, weeks, and even months. Finally, in frustration, I'll abandon the problem as Allyson did and head for the ice cream line. That's why I smiled when I noticed her bunny ears pointing the wrong direction. I could relate.

I wonder how many times I've gone boldly into God's presence with my bunny slippers on the wrong feet, and God has just smiled and hugged me anyway.

God loves us in spite of our shortcomings. Isn't that good news? Even if we have to ask His help and cry out, "Father, which one goes on which foot?" day after day, He will continue to teach us with great patience, love, and understanding. And on the days when we just can't figure it out, even with His coaching, He reaches down and puts the shoes on our feet for us.

I'm sure I make many more mistakes than I even realize, but God is so good and merciful that He covers me and protects me until I finally learn which one goes on which foot. He'll do the same for you.

So if you're struggling with something in your life today, and you just can't figure out which one goes on which foot, God's got you covered. Even if you're in such a mess that you can't even find your bunny slippers, don't worry. No problem, no situation, no challenge is bigger than our God. He loves you and He wants to help. Just ask Him.

THOUGHT for the day: Have you checked your bunny slippers lately? Are you wearing them on the wrong feet? Are you struggling with a situation in life that you can't figure out? Go to God. He wants to help you.

SCRIPTURE reading: Psalm 103; Proverbs 4:5-7; 1 Peter 5:6-7.

DAILY declaration: Father God, I praise You today for Your mercy and goodness that endures forever. Thank You for loving me despite all my short-comings. Thank You for being patient with me as I grow up in You. With Your help, I know I'll be able to figure out which one goes on which foot in every situation in life. I love You.

Chapter Eighteen

I WAS

accidentally
bad today

Learning to Be
Honest with God

I watched as all the other children bounded out of kindergarten. One by one, each energetic child ran to a corresponding parent. I searched through the sea of students for my Allyson. Finally, I saw her blond ponytail bobbing up and down as she rounded the corner of the sidewalk. She saw me, too, only she didn't run to me. Instead, she sort of shuffled over to me, head down, dragging her backpack. Something was obviously wrong.

Slowly, she climbed into our vehicle, slouched down in the backseat, and leaned against the window.

"How was school today?" I asked, glancing at her in the rearview mirror.

"Fine," she mumbled.

"Did you do well on your papers today?"

"Uh huh."

"Did you get to play outside today?"

"Uh huh."

"Was your best buddy there today? What's her name, Autumn?"

"Yep."

I was getting nowhere fast, so I decided to take another approach.

"You know, Ally, if there's something bothering you, you can always talk to me."

Silence filled the car as we drove home. She wasn't talking, and I was out of strategies. So I decided to do what any other sleuth would do. After supper was over, I began investigating. First, I questioned the only witness I knew—Abby, the older sister.

She was at school with her sister all day. Maybe she'll know something, I thought.

"Ab, did something happen to Allyson today?" I asked.

"I don't know," Abby said, never taking her eyes off of the TV. "I hardly saw her today."

Okay, then I'll check her folder for clues, I thought.

I rooted through her backpack, removed every paper from her folder, and came up empty. She'd done really well on all her papers.

What could it be? I wondered. *What could have happened to make her so upset?*

As I shoved her papers back into her dolphin folder, I remembered that I was supposed to sign her daily calendar that was tacked inside her folder. I found a pen in the kitchen junk drawer and moved my finger down the calendar to the correct day. Just as I was about to sign my initials, I saw it. A big yellow dot.

All the other days had green dots on them, but that day had a big yellow dot right in the center of the square. Green meant good behavior; yellow meant bad behavior. And red...well, that meant "you've been so bad that you're getting suspended" behavior.

Thank God it's not a red dot, I thought, trying to humor myself.

The yellow dot glared at me as if to say, "Your little baby isn't so perfect after all. You'd better do something about it. She'll get a reputation for being an ill-behaved child, and then she'll start doing poorly in school. Blah. Blah. Blah."

I just couldn't believe it. Allyson had never been in trouble at school before. She was even awarded the citizenship honor in preschool.

And now, a year later, she's been given a yellow dot!

I was in total shock. I knew I had to deal with the yellow-dot situation, but I sure didn't want to. I drank a diet cola and had a piece of chocolate in the solitude of the kitchen. That always cheered me up. As I drank the last drop of soda, I knew it was time to deal with it.

"Allyson!" I called.

No response.

"Abby, where's your sister?" I asked.

"Her room, I think."

I eased open Ally's bedroom door to discover her lying facedown on her bed. She was listening to one of my Frank Sinatra CDs on the new CD player she'd received for Christmas. Sinatra was crooning "Come Fly with Me," which, of course, I wanted to do rather than deal with the yellow-dot dilemma.

I turned down the music and sat on the side of her bed.

"Ally, honey, I know about the yellow dot," I said, stroking her hair.

She jerked away from me and hid her face in a nearby pillow.

"Do you want to tell me what happened, or do I have to call your teacher?"

That comment struck a nerve. She shot up off that pillow and pleaded with me. "No, Mommy, please don't call her."

"Well, then, what happened?"

Allyson hesitated for a moment, and then she looked up at me with her big, blue, teary eyes and said, "I was accidentally bad today."

I had to hold back the laughter. That was a new one, even for Allyson.

"How were you accidentally bad?" I asked with raised eyebrows.

With tears streaming down her face, she unloaded the whole story.

"I was listening to Ms. Barbara, but then Autumn told me something, and I said something back, and Ms. Barbara told us to be quiet. But we just kept talking, so Ms. Barbara made us move away from each other. Then I couldn't talk to Autumn anymore, so I made funny faces at her, and she made funny faces back and made me laugh, and Ms. Barbara got mad because we weren't listening, and we got in trouble. I just couldn't help it, Mommy!"

With that, Allyson collapsed onto her pillow and sobbed uncontrollably. She came up for air long enough to blurt out, "I didn't mean to. I didn't mean to change my dot to yellow. I'm sorry, Mommy."

"It's okay, Allyson," I comforted. "Everyone makes mistakes once in a while. Just try not to be accidentally bad tomorrow."

I kissed her on the head, turned up Frank, and left her alone in her room. There was no need to punish her. She'd already punished herself enough. I was pretty sure she wouldn't misbehave again and risk another yellow-dot episode.

Later, as I replayed the event for Jeff, we both had a good laugh over Allyson's remark: "I was accidentally bad today." It was so funny. It was so creative. It was so ridiculous. It was...so something I would say to God.

The more I thought about it, the more I realized how often I'd tried that same line on God. I would go to prayer, fully intending to repent for my misdeeds, but instead I would come up with something like: "God, I know I acted awful today, but I didn't mean to. I didn't get much sleep last night, and I was sort of grouchy all day. It wasn't my intention to be like that, really."

Never once in that prayer would I actually say, "I repent for my inexcusable behavior. I'm truly sorry, Lord. Please forgive me." Nope, I would try to make some really good excuses, add a few tears, and hope for the best.

Through Allyson's yellow-dot experience, I realized that my pitiful prayer full of weak excuses was no better than Allyson's "I was accidentally bad today" alibi. In fact, it was worse. At least her excuse was sort of funny. Mine was putrid in God's eyes, and I knew it. Every time I had used that sort of excuse-ridden prayer, I always felt worse afterward.

Then, like Allyson, guilt would overtake me, and I'd bury my head in my pillow and sob. But you know what? All of those "feel sorry for myself tears" didn't do me a bit of good. It wasn't until I came to the Father in honesty and truly repented for my poor behavior that the guilt feelings left me and peace flooded my heart once again.

That's when God would stroke my hair and say, "It's okay, Michelle. Everyone makes mistakes once in a while. Just try not to be accidentally bad tomorrow."

I'd eventually take my head out of my pillow, wipe my eyes, and determine to go for the green dot. I was no longer satisfied to get a yellow dot. Nothing was worth being out of fellowship with my Father.

If you've been making excuses when you go to God in prayer, it's time to get honest before Him. He's not a big, mean God who is ready to whop you on the head every time you act ugly. You don't have to be afraid to be honest with Him. He already knows the truth anyway, so tell your Heavenly Father the real story. Confess your sin and ask for His forgiveness. As soon as you repent, He casts it in the sea of forgetfulness, never to be brought up again. So if you've been accidentally bad today, God doesn't want your excuses. He just wants your honesty.

THOUGHT for the day: Have you been making excuses instead of being honest with God?

SCRIPTURE reading: Romans 7:14-25; 2 Corinthians 5:17-21; 1 John 1:9.

DAILY declaration: Father, I come to You today in total honesty. I repent, Father. I don't have any more excuses, Lord. I am truly sorry and ready to move forward with You. I want to walk with You, Lord. I want to go for the green dot every day. And if I miss it from time to time, I want to be honest enough to come before You, knowing that You'll forgive me and love me as I am transformed from glory to glory. Amen.

Chapter Nineteen

LOOK,

mommy! a dalmatian cow!

Seeing Things
Through a Child's Eyes

It had been one of those days. One of the dogs had thrown up on the living room carpet. My editor had passed me over for a major project and assigned it to one of my co-workers. The air-conditioning in our SUV had gone out. And I'd spilled orange pop all over the front of my white blouse. I just wanted to go home, put on a T-shirt and shorts, and relax in the recliner.

My mind replayed the day as the girls and I headed home. I was caught up in the "woe is me" mode when my thoughts were interrupted by a high-pitched squeal coming from the backseat.

"Look, Mommy!" Allyson shrieked with glee.

"What, honey? Look at what?" I asked, glancing out my side window to see a field full of Holstein cows.

"Look, Mommy! A Dalmatian cow!" she said.

It took a moment for my mind to process what she'd said—a Dalmatian cow.

"Oh, you mean those black-and-white cows in that field?" I asked, trying not to laugh.

"Uh huh," she said excitedly. "I've never seen a Dalmatian cow before. They must only have them in Texas."

"You're probably right," I played along. "Those Dalmatian cows sure are neat."

"Can we get one?" Abby chimed in.

"No, we don't have anyplace to keep a cow," I answered. "Besides, you've got two dachshunds at home who would be very jealous if you gave all of your love to a Dalmatian cow."

"Okay," Abby said. "We won't get one."

As soon as I got home, I called my parents to share with them Allyson's unique observation. We all had a good laugh about the field full of Dalmatian cows.

Kids are funny, I thought. *They see things in such a different light.*

As I loaded the dishwasher that evening, still feeling a little depressed about my terrible day, my mind kept drifting back to Allyson's Dalmatian cows. The more I thought about it, the more I realized there was much to be learned from her funny comment.

I looked out the window, and all I saw was a field full of Holstein cows—a sight I'd seen hundreds of times in my life—so I didn't give it a second thought. And I certainly didn't appreciate it. But Allyson did. She looked at the same field and rejoiced over Dalmatian cows. I could feel the Holy Spirit's presence as I continued down that path of thought.

It was the old "glass half empty or half full" concept. Shamefully, I realized I'd been guilty of looking at that glass and saying, "That glass is half empty. There's not enough water in there to satisfy me. I want more," instead of being appreciative of the existing water in the glass.

I realized that it had been a long time since I'd been truly thankful for anything that God had done for me. Sure, I praised Him a little every day during my quiet time, but I certainly wasn't looking for new reasons to sing His praises. In other words, I wasn't searching fields of cows for reasons to appreciate Him.

I determined in my heart to make a change that very moment. First, I told the Lord I was sorry for taking His beautiful creation for granted.

"I'll be more observant and appreciative," I prayed. "Help me, Lord, to see things as Allyson does. Help me to be quick to notice the good things You've done."

Then I began praising Him for the many blessings in my life. As I praised Him for my Godly husband, my two precious children, my wonderful parents and in-laws, my sister and brother and their families, our good health, our home—the fog began to lift.

I kept praising Him: "Father, I thank You for protecting us from the tornadoes that ripped through our city last month. Lord, I thank You for blessing my children with wonderful teachers. I praise You that a front row parking space opened up for me at the grocery store yesterday...."

The more I praised, the more the disappointment and discouragement I'd felt earlier that day drifted away. By filling my mouth with praise, my heart was filled with peace. So I kept on.

"Lord, I praise You for butterflies and ladybugs. I praise You for the sunshine today. I thank You for sending Abby and Allyson nice friends in their new

school. I praise You that I was able to find our lawn
furniture on clearance...."

After thirty minutes or so, I was so excited, I almost
squealed as Allyson had when she saw the cows. I felt like
a new person. Suddenly, I could see how blessed I was. It
was as if God had lifted the blinders from my eyes and I
was seeing the world around me in a newer, clearer way.
I never wanted to lose that perspective again.

Am I singing God's praises all of the time? I wish I
could answer yes, but I'm not there yet. However, I am a
lot better than I used to be about thanking my Lord for
all that He does.

I attended a women's Bible study not long ago, and the
woman leading the session challenged each of us to keep a
praise notebook. She said that she had begun doing that,
and it had drawn her much closer to the Father.

"Just list four or five things that God does for you
each day," she encouraged. "Ask God to help you be
more observant of His blessings."

I can do that, I thought.

So that's what I've been doing. I have a little red
notebook that I refer to as my Notebook O' Praise. Its
edges are a little tattered because I carry it with me in
my purse (and the inside of my purse is a scary place to
be), but it's priceless to me. You know why? Because I
can look back over the past months and read about all of
the blessings the Father has performed in my life. I
might have forgotten some of the smaller things if I
hadn't recorded them in my notebook, but now I'll never
forget them.

If I am having one of those days when the dog has
thrown up on the carpet or my editor has rejected one of
my articles, I get out my Notebook O' Praise and read a
few pages. As I do, the fog lifts, and I'm walking in
sunshine once again.

I encourage you to get yourself a Notebook O' Praise
and begin recording every little thing that God does for
you. I've cut out a picture of a Dalmatian cow and put it
on the inside cover of my notebook, but you don't have
to unless you want to.

If you've been one of those "glass half empty"
people, that can change today. Right now, wherever you
are, just raise your hands to the Father and praise Him
for who He is and all He's done. Pretty soon, the fog
will lift in your life, and you're likely to see some
Dalmatian cows, too.

THOUGHT for the day: Have you
become a "glass half empty" person? When was the last
time you really praised the Lord?

SCRIPTURE reading: Psalms 9:1-2;
107:1-2; 147:1; 150.

DAILY declaration: Father God, I praise You today for who You are and all that You've done for me. You alone, God, are worthy of praise. I want You to know how much I appreciate all that You do for me every day. Lord, help me to be more mindful of Your great works in the world around me. Help me to never take for granted the many things You do. Make my eyes observant of Your goodness, Lord. I want to give You all of the praise that You so rightly deserve. I love You, Lord. I praise Your Holy Name!

Chapter Twenty

YOU'RE

the worst picker-outer in the whole world!

Giving Your Children to God

Getting ready to go anywhere had become quite a sight to behold in the Adams' household. As my husband, Jeff, always says, "Three women getting ready in the same bathroom is a scary thing!"

Blow dryers, curling irons, hot rollers, hair spray, lotions, perfumes, glitter gel, nail files, nail polish, makeup, bows, barrettes, brushes, jewelry—all important parts of the daily grooming routine—were scattered across the master bathroom.

Jeff waited his turn outside the bathroom with his only ally—Miller, our little dachshund. It was safer out there.

An hour later, we were all sprayed, spritzed, and sparkly. All we lacked were a few finishing touches.

"Come here, Ab," I called to her across the bathroom. "I want to put this bow in your hair."

"Mother!" she protested. "I am *not* wearing a bow. Bows are for babies. I want to wear a headband. Those are in, you know."

"Yes, Abby, I am well aware that headbands are hip and happening, but I think a bow will look more ladylike with your Sunday dress."

As I snapped the bow into place, Abby made a face of agony in the mirror.

"I look stupid."

"No, you look adorable," I encouraged.

"Mom, I'm not a baby anymore. Bows are for babies!"

"Abby, I am thirty years old, and I know a thing or two about what looks good and what doesn't, and I am telling you that bows are not just for babies," I retorted in my motherly tone. "I mean, I even wear bows when I put my hair in a low ponytail. Do you think I'm a baby?"

To that, Abby rolled her eyes, sighed, and left the bathroom in total frustration.

I had won, but I had a feeling the war was far from over.

I was right.

Minutes later, Abby reappeared holding seven different headbands. She had sparkly ones, pearl ones, silver and gold ones, and fabric ones.

"See, Mom, I have headbands that match this dress," she explained, "and this pearl one is very dressy, don't you think?"

To that, *I* rolled my eyes, sighed, and removed the bow from her hair.

"Fine. Wear the pearl one," I said, hesitating. "Allyson can wear the bow."

Allyson took one look at my frustrated face and decided cooperation with Mom was definitely the best option. So Abby wore her precious headband, and Allyson wore the stupid bow. I was halfway happy as we headed to church.

At ages seven and five, Abby and Allyson were very particular about the way they looked. They each had very distinctive opinions about what was cool and what was not. Much of the time, anything I liked fell into the latter category. So I chose my battles wisely, and the rest of the time, I let the girls make their own choices about their hair, clothes, and accessories to achieve their own personal "look." (Of course, I drew the line when Ally wanted to wear her ballerina outfit to school, but normally, they do an okay job.)

In fact, at times, Ab had more fashion sense and style than I'd ever had, and she was quick to tell me when I'd made a fashion faux pas in her eyes. Like the time when I wore a leopard-print tank top that was actually part of a pajama set I owned. I wore the tank with a pair of black jeans and a black jacket, thinking I looked pretty stylish until Abby took one look at me and said, "You're not wearing that are you!" Or there was the time when I wore my military-inspired blazer, and Abby wanted to know if the decorative buttons were ones I'd earned in Girl Scouts.

The girls weren't always as "with it" as they believed, but I took some of their fashion advice to heart. I've discovered that one is never too old to learn a thing or two. However, there are a few fashion rules that I know from years of dressing myself—rules that are foreign to Abby and Allyson at their young ages. Those are the rules that sometimes cause fashion feuds in our home.

One such event took place on a sunny February Sunday morning. As I helped Allyson buckle her dress shoes, I noticed that Abby was putting on shoes that I hadn't picked out for her.

"Ab, where are your black dress shoes?" I asked.

"In my closet."

"Why aren't they on your feet?" I asked, staring at the white patent leather sandals she had obviously chosen.

"Because white goes better with my dress," Abby explained.

"But, Abby, it's too early in the year to wear white. It's still winter. Besides, your feet will get cold. You need to wear your black shoes."

"But, Mom, black doesn't go with pink," Abby protested.

"That's not true," I said. "Black goes with every-thing. They'll look beautiful with your dress. Now go put them on."

"Uggghhhhh," Abby groaned. "You are the worst picker-outer in the whole world!"

Well, I'd held many titles in my lifetime, but "worst picker-outer" was a new one. Halfway amused and halfway offended, I went to the car to wait to for the rest of the family.

Why won't she trust me? I thought. *Does she really think I'd let her wear something that would make her look foolish? Doesn't she know that I really do know best? Doesn't she respect me anymore? Why does she constantly challenge me?*

The questions flooded my mind. And just as I was about to answer the questions myself, lick my wounds, and pout a while, God interrupted me.

This is just the beginning.

The beginning of what? I thought.

*Your girls are going to make their own decisions on many
things in life—things much more important than fashion—
and you won't always be able to make them do what you want
them to do.*

That scared me. I knew it was true. At ages seven and
five, I still had control, but the time was coming when I
wouldn't have that total control, and it was coming more
quickly than I liked.

You are going to have to give them to Me.

I was somewhat hurt by God's words to me. I
thought I had already given my daughters to Him. I
mean, I had even spoken those very words at their baby
dedications in front of a whole assembly of people.

The Holy Spirit began ministering to me, showing
me that I hadn't really given them to God. I let God
borrow them from time to time, but I had always taken
them back.

Why would I do that? I questioned.

I heard the word "fear" rise up inside of me.

It was true. I was afraid to totally give my children to
God, thinking He might not parent them as well as I
could. Isn't that ridiculous thinking? It was much more
ridiculous than Abby not trusting me to know which
shoes looked best with her pink dress, though I hated to
admit it.

During those few minutes alone in the car, I cried
out to God.

"I trust You, God, but what if You call them to
foreign countries to be missionaries? What if You call
them into dangerous professions? What if...."

Then I heard God's tender voice in my mind, asking of me, the very questions I'd asked about Abby moments before: *Why won't she trust Me? Doesn't she know that I really do know best? Doesn't she respect Me anymore? Why does she constantly challenge Me?*

That day, sitting in the car by myself, I truly gave my girls to God. It was one of the hardest things I have ever done, and it continues to be difficult. I find that I have to give them to Him daily, because if I don't, I'll take them right back again.

I realize that Abby and Allyson won't always make decisions that I agree with or even approve of, but who's to say that I'm always going to be right? I miss it sometimes, even when my intentions are good. It's bad enough when I miss it and a poor decision affects me, but I don't think I could stand knowing that one of my poor decisions adversely affected my girls.

When I really think about it, it's a big relief to put that responsibility back on God's shoulders. By giving my girls to God, I don't have to worry about "missing it" where they're concerned because He is in control of their lives. If they make a mistake, I might not be able to fix it, but God can, and He promises that He will.

I can't see the future, but God can, and He is already preparing Abby and Allyson for what He has called them to do in life. No matter how much I love my girls, I could never guide them as well as He can, because I don't know the things that He knows. I can't be everywhere they are, but God can. So you see, giving our children to God is the best thing we could ever do for them.

If you're struggling with this same issue, don't fight it any longer. Don't be afraid. Just give your children to God. I don't care if your kids are seven or seventy, it's never too late to turn them over to your Heavenly Father.

Maybe your children have drifted away from God. They may even be caught up in the world's way of thinking. Perhaps they are even involved in some serious sin situations right now. It doesn't matter—God is bigger than all of that. You can't fix it. I bet you've tried because you love them so much, but God is our wonderful redeemer. In fact, when God repairs a situation, He restores it better than it was in its original state. That's just the kind of God He is—incredible and merciful.

So give your children over to Him today. And even if they choose to wear white sandals in the middle of winter, God will keep their feet warm.

THOUGHT for the day: Have you really given your kids to God?

SCRIPTURE reading: 1 Samuel, chapter 1.

DAILY declaration: Lord, I realize that I haven't totally given my children to You. I have been holding back out of fear, but, Lord, I'm not afraid any longer. I trust You with even my most precious treasures—my children. This very day, I give them to You—100 percent. Thank You, Lord, for loving my children even more than I do. Amen.

epilogue

Growing Up Together

People used to say to me, "Enjoy it while your kids are young, because these are the best days of your life."

I'd smile and nod my head as the smell of baby spit-up filled my nostrils and a forty-pound diaper bag pained my shoulder.

Are they kidding? I would think. *Is this really as good as it gets?*

Then, as time marched on, my babies became toddlers. I'd see those same people at a local store, and they'd say the same thing, "Enjoy them while they're young because these are the best days of your life."

I'd try to listen as Allyson rolled on the floor in a "terrible two's temper tantrum" and Abby pulled over an entire rack of greeting cards.

"Uh huh, I know," I'd say, rolling my eyes as I walked off.

Then my girls entered preschool and now elementary school. The same people keep saying the same thing, but I'm not the same. All of sudden, I believe them! These really are the best days of my life.

Every day that I have with my daughters is a gift from God. I am realizing that more and more as they grow up more quickly than I'd like. We're long past the baby bottles, diapers, pacifiers, and Barney stage—a stage I longed to get out of. But you know what? Those were precious times. I just didn't realize that when I was up to my eyeballs in dirty diapers.

But now I don't take each day for granted. No, I treasure every moment with them—even the mad fits and time-outs. I don't want to miss a single moment of their growing up. As they mature physically, I am maturing spiritually. God is using them to teach me so many things. We are growing up together, and in the process, we are growing so close to one another. I know there are many more lessons ahead, and I look forward to every one.

end notes

[1] Sandy Gills, *Mr. Francis' Wife* (Colorado Springs, CO: Chariot Victor Publishing, 1998), 170.

about the author

Michelle Medlock Adams has had a
passion for writing since she was a small
child. When other children were outside
playing, Michelle was often found curled up
under a tree with a notebook and pencil in
hand. That love for writing continued to
grow, and it wasn't long before her writing
began to earn notable recognition.

    Michelle has won several literary awards as a book author
and a former reporter for the Bedford (Indiana) Times-Mail
newspaper, including first place recognition from the
Associated Press and the Society of Professional Journalists.
She is a frequent contributor to a variety of magazines and
newspapers around the country, as well as, the author of
dozens of gift, devotional, and children's picture books.

    Because of her enthusiasm for life and natural gift of pres-
entation, Michelle is often sought after as a devotional and
public speaker to special interest groups around the country.

    As a working mother with two energetic daughters, she is
uniquely qualified to write this book! She enjoys life with her
husband, Jeff, "her hero," their daughters, Abby and Allyson,
and their three miniature dachshunds.

    For additional information on seminars, scheduling speak-
ing engagements, or to write the author, please send your
correspondence to: iufan@michellemedlockadams.com

This and other titles by White Stone Books
are available from your local bookstore.

Visit our Web site at:
www.whitestonebooks.com

If this book has touched your life
we would love to hear from you.
Please write us at:
White Stone Books
Department E
1501 South Florida Avenue
Lakeland, Florida 33803

"… To him who overcomes I will give
some of the hidden manna to eat.
And I will give him a white stone, and on
the stone a new name written which no one
knows except him who receives it."
Revelation 2:17 NKJV

WHITE STONE BOOKS
LAKELAND, FLORIDA